1 ̣₂₉₅

Unlocking the Cabinet

Unlocking the Cabinet
Cabinet Structures in Comparative Perspective

Edited by
Thomas T. Mackie
Brian W. Hogwood

SAGE Modern Politics Series Volume 10
Sponsored by the European Consortium for Political
Research/ECPR

SAGE Publications · London · Beverly Hills · New Delhi

SAGE Publications Ltd
28 Banner Street
London EC1Y 8QE

 SAGE Publications Inc
275 South Beverly Drive
Beverly Hills, California 90212

SAGE Publications India Pvt Ltd
C-236 Defence Colony
New Delhi 110 024

British Library Cataloguing in Publication Data

Mackie, Thomas T. (Thomas Taylor)
   Unlocking the cabinet: cabinet structures in
   comparative perspective.—(E.C.P.R. modern
   politics series; 10)
   1. Cabinet systems   2. Comparative government
   I. Title   II. Hogwood, Brian W.   III. Series
   351.004   JF331

ISBN 0-8039-9724-8
ISBN 0-8039-9725-6 Pbk

Library of Congress catalog card number 85-062173

Printed in Great Britain by
J.W. Arrowsmith Ltd, Bristol

Contents

Preface

Our original intention in carrying out the research which led to this book was simply to explore the extent to which different countries made information about cabinet committees easily available, and in particular whether Britain was unusually secretive. We would like to thank Peter Hennessy for the original inspiration which set us off on this quest and for his continuing interest since. Our finding was that Britain is much more secretive than other countries, though the announcement of the names and chairmanship of four standing committees in 1979 and again in 1983 marked a greater though still limited degree of openness. We asked the embassies or high commissions of the countries concerned whether they had cabinet committees and, if so, to provide us with a list of all of them. Almost all of them provided this information willingly, and in a number of cases provided us with considerable additional material, in some cases even putting us in touch with their cabinet offices. In this book we have also been able to draw on the special knowledge of the authors of the individual country chapters in part II.

We would like to thank all those who have commented on the various drafts of our work on cabinet committees which eventually led to the first four chapters of this book.

A workshop on cabinet committees at the ECPR Joint Sessions at Freiburg in March 1983 enabled us to gather together authors from a number of countries. We are grateful to all those who participated in the workshop and in particular to those who revised their papers for inclusion in this book. A very special thanks is due to those who did not participate in that meeting but were nevertheless willing to contribute chapters specifically for this book.

I
CABINET STRUCTURES IN COMPARATIVE PERSPECTIVE

1
Decision-making in cabinet government

Thomas T. Mackie and Brian W. Hogwood

1.1 Cabinet structures: a neglected but important theme

The roles played by cabinet structures in the decision-making of political executives is an oddly neglected subject in the comparative study of politics. Both formal institutions and less formal mechanisms in arriving at decisions in political executives are surprisingly understudied. There have been some important comparative studies of political executives but these have tended to focus on the role of the head of the political executive — the president or prime minister (see especially Rose and Suleiman, 1980). The distinctive nature of cabinet systems as against presidential systems has been well brought out (Rose, 1980) but a comparative framework for the analysis of variations among cabinet systems in the role of decision arenas other than the full cabinet has not previously been developed. Blondel (1980) in his wide-ranging survey of government structures gives only a passing mention to cabinet committees. Accordingly what started out on our part as a research interest in cabinet committees, developed into a framework of decision arenas in cabinet systems.

This book is concerned with decision-making *within* political executives in cabinet systems. It is not concerned as such with broader government-society links, such as the role of interest groups, or 'corporatism', except in so far as these are reflected in the mechanisms for handling decisions within the executive. Nor does the book focus on the determination of decision-making roles within departments, e.g. ministerial-civil service relationships, though it does discuss civil service back-up for cabinet and cabinet committees and the roles of interdepartmental committees of civil servants (see especially chapter 2).

1

Studying the structure of executives — the number of committees and the formal allocation of their membership and responsibilities — is of interest as evidence of how government organizes itself to coordinate its tasks (both in the senses of ensuring consultation and resolving conflicts). These structures are examined in chapter 2. However, this does not by itself tell us much about processes within the cabinet structure. For example, cabinet committees in a number of countries studied are technically only discussion committees, with the full cabinet formally taking decisions. Yet the reality may be that such cabinet committees frequently take the effective decision, with cabinets merely endorsing or legitimating committee decisions. A number of countries (Britain, Australia, New Zealand) recognize this practical reality by limiting the opportunity to reopen in full cabinet matters resolved in committees and giving committee decisions the same formal authority as the minutes of the full cabinet. However, the study of the relationship between the committees and cabinet is too narrow a focus within which to examine the role of committees in coordination and the resolution of conflicts at the centre of government. Committees and the full cabinet are only two of the many arenas within which decisions taken in the name of the government as a whole are actually resolved.

Rather than attempt to give country-by-country analyses of the formal and informal processes within the cabinet system or attempt generalizations which may conceal important variations between countries, we feel it would be more useful to present a comparative framework within which differences between countries can be explored. Any such comparative framework, in addition to enabling ready comparisons between countries, should also enable comparison across time and comparisons between different policy areas within a single country. We would expect policy areas to vary in the extent to which decisions about them are taken in particular arenas. For example, the locations of decision-making about foreign policy are likely to differ from those affecting, say, energy policy.

Our comparative framework is based on a classification of the different arenas, both institutionalized and informal, within which members of cabinet may arrive at what are effectively final government decisions, though these may subsequently have to be formally endorsed by full cabinet. These arenas, listed below, are categories potentially applicable to all parliamentary systems, and thus provide a comparative framework for analysing intra-executive relations generally in those countries.

The various possible arenas for decision-making are:

(1) *unilateral decisions*, taken by a minister as head of a

department or by other ministers or officials within his or her department;

(2) *'internalized' coordination*, where a minister heading more than one department effectively acts as a one-person cabinet committee;

(3) *bilateral decisions*, resulting from discussions between pairs of ministers, such as the budget minister and the head of a spending department;

(4) *multilateral decisions*, involving discussions or negotiations among a number of ministers outside a formal committee framework;

(5) *cabinet committee decisions*, where the effective decision is taken at the committee rather than full cabinet;

(6) *cabinet decisions*, where the full cabinet takes the effective decision on matters referred to it directly or issues already considered by cabinet committees;

(7) *party decision*, where the effective decision is taken as a result of inter (or intra) party negotiations, for example, among ministers in a coalition acting as members of their party rather than as departmental heads or cabinet ministers.

This typology of arenas does not exhaust the possibility of interaction among members of cabinets. Informal and personal links may be very important in determining which ministers speak together about what outside cabinet, and how they form alliances within cabinet, as numerous memoirs of members of British cabinets attest (see, for example, Wilson, 1971; Crossman, 1975, 1976, 1977; Castle, 1980). Where such informal groups consist of a select group of senior ministers meeting with the prime minister they are often referred to as 'inner cabinets' (and in the case of the 1964–70 Wilson government in Britain this was formalized into a committee). No attempt will be made here to explore fully such personal and informal links. Where such links do contribute to the making of a decision, it will normally be within one of the arenas described above.

In this chapter we outline the roles played by various decision arenas in cabinet governments. In chapter 2 we describe which countries have cabinet committees, their number and functions and their establishment and composition. Chapter 3 analyses the pattern of fragmented but overlapping decision arenas which appear typical of cabinet systems. Part II of this book examines the cabinet structures in a number of individual countries.

1.2 Unilateral

Most government decisions are made within the confines of single government departments. Most of these are, of course, detailed decisions about the implementation of agreed government policy. Such decisions can, however, be quite important individually.

The extent to which important decisions, including policy decisions, can be made within individual departments will vary according to a number of factors, including the way in which portfolios were initially divided up and intrinsic characteristics of the functions of the department which will determine the extent to which they interact with the functions of other departments. Chapter 4 on the United Kingdom shows how the education department and the Home Office (dealing mostly with law and order issues) were relatively self-contained (as long as no political blunders were made), while the work of the trade department interacted with many other departments. The work of a budget ministry is intrinsically interdepartmental, with the ministry having both to bargain bilaterally about departmental allocations and seek collective agreement to overall ceilings.

In contrasting decisions involving a single department with those involving a number, we are not arguing that only actors within the individual department are necessarily involved: decision-making is often less than strictly unilateral: it is often the product of negotiation between a department and relevant groups.

Even if a matter is within a minister's own authority to take a decision the minister may well seek to raise a matter in full cabinet. For example, in Australia, by informing cabinet colleagues of his or her intention, the minister can act in the knowledge that colleagues have had an opportunity to express a view on that decision. Similar occasions occur in New Zealand or Britain. However, other cabinet members may be irritated if used too much as a 'political comfort station' in this manner when responsibility for the decision lies clearly with the individual minister.

Cabinets and their associated committees are not devices which attempt to suck all important ministerial decisions in for collective decision-making. On the contrary, they adopt filters to keep as many issues as possible off the cabinet agenda. One such filter is a reluctance to take up issues which are within the scope of an individual minister's remit. Such a filter may not be wholly effective if a minister prefers the reassurance of his or her colleagues' support, but in larger countries, at least, a minister would meet resistance to trying to place items unnecessarily on the cabinet agenda.

1.3 Internalized coordination
Unilateral decisions referred to those decisions made within a single department, often by the minister, but there is not necessarily a

one-to-one relationship between ministers and departments. Countries with small numbers of ministers may appoint the same minister to head a number of departments. Where these departments are functionally interrelated, there is scope for the minister to carry out an internalized interdepartmental coordinating role, dealing with issues which might otherwise have to go to cabinet or cabinet committee. For example, in Luxembourg in 1979 the same minister headed both the finance and the labour and social security departments, while another minister headed both the transport and energy and the posts and telecommunications departments. However, another minister headed the not obviously related armed forces and public health departments, so the evidence suggests that multi-departmental ministers are not systematically used as a coordinating device. In Britain, between 1962 to 1964 the same minister headed the Commonwealth relations and colonies departments (which were later merged), but this is an isolated example.

Even when the appearance of internalized coordination exists it may be a continuation of unilateral decision-making. In Ireland, for example, the number of ministers is constitutionally limited to fifteen while the number of ministries is eighteen, so some ministers must have responsibility for more than one department. However, even where those departments are functionally interrelated decision-making may rest with the separate departments. In the 1973–7 government the same minister was responsible for both the Department of Health and the Department of Social Welfare, but his junior minister was in effect in charge of the latter department (Gallagher, 1980).

Occasionally, prime ministers have attempted to introduce individual ministers as coordinators over departments headed by other ministers. One such attempt was the introduction by Churchill in Britain of a number of 'overlords' responsible for coordinating a number of related departments (Gordon Walker, 1972; Jones, 1975). An important difference between these 'overlords' and the multi-departmental ministers discussed in the previous paragraph is that the 'overlords' were appointed on top of the existing departmental ministers rather than being heads of departments themselves. As Blondel (1982: 152) concludes after reviewing the experience of 'super ministers' in Britain and France:

in the final analysis, departments have to be abolished if superministers are truly to coordinate the activities of a broad sector of government. Otherwise, coordination occurs, whether there are superministers or not, by the traditional method of consultation and committee decision-making.

1.4 **Bilateral**

Many of the key decisions affecting a department, namely those concerning programme finance, are the subject of bilateral negotiation between the spending department and the budget ministry. The full cabinet may determine the ceiling within which allocations are to be made and perhaps set broad guidelines, and it (or a special cabinet committee) may act as a court of appeal where the spending department and the budget ministry are unable to reach agreement, but the cabinet will not normally review allocations which have been agreed in bilateral negotiations between spending departments and the budget ministry. Only when there is a political row following the announcement, as described in chapter 4 on Britain, will the issue then be reopened, and even then the subsequent further decision may not be taken in full cabinet.

Another important set of bilateral links within the cabinet framework is between the prime minister and a few key ministers, normally the budget and finance or economic affairs ministries and the foreign ministry. An extreme example of a close, exclusive bilateral relationship between prime minister and finance minister is that between the British prime minister and the Chancellor of the Exchequer over the annual taxation changes (see chapter 4). Prime ministers tend to devote a much larger proportion of their item to foreign affairs than to the work of other departments and many issues may be discussed between the prime minister and the foreign minister without ever being brought to the attention of other ministers (see, e.g., Rose, 1980: 335–8; Gordon Walker, 1972: 88, 116).

1.5 **Multilateral**

Here we are concerned with decisions arrived at through discussions among a number of ministries but outside the formal cabinet committee structure. Informal discussions, agreements and anticipated reaction appear to be particularly important in small countries such as Norway and Ireland but exist in all countries regardless of the extent of cabinet committees. Clearly, for countries without a system of cabinet committees such arrangements may serve as a substitute. In Sweden, an 'even less formal kind of Cabinet decision making is that of two or three ministers concerned discussing the matter — with or without the presence of subordinate officials from their ministries — in order to reach agreement, without taking up the time of the Cabinet as a whole' (Vinde and Petri, 1978). This example indicates that countries which do without cabinet committees still require the development of less formal mechanisms to handle complex problems.

Relatively informal methods of reaching agreement are also very important in small countries, such as Norway and Ireland, which do have a few committees. Referring to Norway, Olsen (1980: 238) states: 'The communications network is primarily characterised by clusters of contact among three or four ministries, the functional equivalent to non-existent formal cabinet committees.' In Ireland there are very few formal committees. Meetings of ministers, even if they recur, are best not described as committees, since they are so informal.

It is, however, important not to regard informal multilateral arrangements and cabinet committees as mutually exclusive. In Britain there is a complex network of interdepartmental committees outside the cabinet committee structure, mainly interdepartmental committees of officials rather than ministers, and in addition there is a considerable amount of interministerial correspondence.

Australia also has a fully ramified cabinet committee structure, but multilateral decision-making can be important. For example, in November 1983 the Australian Labor Prime Minister, Bob Hawke, and his foreign minister and defence minister endorsed the decision of the previous Liberal Fraser government to cooperate with the United States in the testing of MX missiles in international waters to the east of Australia (*Financial Times*, 7 February 1985). This decision was not considered by the full cabinet and, indeed, only became fully public at the beginning of 1985. The decision was strongly opposed by the left of the Labor Party and the prime minister decided, apparently unilaterally, to reverse the policy of cooperating with the tests. This in turn angered other ministers who had not been consulted, including the foreign minister. The full cabinet subsequently endorsed Mr Hawke's action, but only after being presented with a *fait accompli*. This example shows how the same issue can go through different arenas at different times for different decisions relating to it.

1.6 Cabinet committees

The various coordinating and decision-making mechanisms described above are insufficient to reduce the burden on full cabinet in most countries. Thus a formal system of cabinet committees is required. Such cabinet committees could in practice perform a variety of different roles, with the same committee performing different roles in relation to different decisions.

Discussions between departments in preparation for cabinet committees may lead to consensus so that the committee meeting itself may merely endorse the decision. Such decisions would invariably not be discussed by full cabinet, so here it is effectively the cabinet committee which is performing the 'legitimating' role.

Cabinet committees may fail to agree sufficiently to arrive at a final decision; however, even here the cabinet committee will have played an important role in defining the issues and narrowing the options for the full cabinet. It will rarely be the argument in the cabinet committee itself that will determine how ministers line up on an issue; the ministers in dispute (if any) will already have evolved their views and ministers not directly involved tend to follow the line of their briefs, at least in the United Kingdom (see, e.g., Barnett, 1982; Kaufman, 1981).

Cabinet committees may arrive at agreement but these decisions may be subject to review by full cabinet. Cabinet cannot possibly give full consideration to all issues already considered in a large number of cabinet committees, and in consequence most decisions, even under a system where all committee decisions are in principle reviewable, will in practice be 'nodded through' the full cabinet. It is worth noting that during the period 1972–5 when Australian cabinet committee decisions were reviewable by the full cabinet over 80 per cent of committee decisions were confirmed by cabinet (Smith, 1976: 209). After 1975 the cabinet reverted to the system of treating standing cabinet committee decisions as having equal authority with decisions of the full cabinet without having to be referred to cabinet (Yeend, 1979).

Constitutionally the most significant role for cabinet committees is where their decisions are treated as final without any reference to cabinet and where these decisions are given equal authority with full cabinet decisions. Only those decisions where agreement cannot be reached are discussed in full cabinet. This is the system which operates in Britain, Australia, New Zealand and Canada.

The roles which cabinet committees will perform will in part depend on the extent of interdepartmental and party disagreements within the government and on informal procedures which have grown up over the years. However, an institutional framework as complex as a cabinet committee structure will normally be regulated by at least some formal written rules defining the relationship between cabinet committees and full cabinet, the status of cabinet committee decisions, and the circumstances under which matters considered by cabinet committees must be taken to the full cabinet. Such rules may be gathered together in the form of a 'Cabinet Manual' as in Britain, Australia, New Zealand and Canada. It is important to distinguish such *operating rules* from *constitutional* provisions (whether written or unwritten). The constitution may prescribe the cabinet as the only body competent to make collective decisions on behalf of the executive, but the operating rules may be that cabinet committees *de facto* have such authority.

In Britain each prime minister may lay down his or her own (unpublished) rules, but the reality of practice in most recent governments appears to be encapsulated by the ruling in 1967 by the then Prime Minister, Harold Wilson, that a matter could be taken to the cabinet from a committee only with the agreement of the committee chairman (who is appointed by the prime minister). In theory, ministers still had the constitutional right to bring any matter to the cabinet, including a question settled in a committee, but 'in practice this right was greatly attenuated' (Gordon Walker, 1972: 44).

Australia and New Zealand accord similar status to their cabinet committees, and since they are more open in making information available about cabinet committees than Britain, it is possible to refer to procedures as set out in the cabinet manuals themselves. The terms of reference of New Zealand cabinet committees appended to the Cabinet Office Manual give them power to take decisions which are reported each week to Cabinet 'for noting — rather than for endorsement or confirmation (which would tend to detract from their delegated authority)' (New Zealand Cabinet Office, n.d., ch. D, para. 4.1). The *principle* of cabinet responsibility is retained because the cabinet retains the 'ultimate power of decision and can direct a committee to review a decision or can itself reverse it', but the terms of reference underline the decision-making autonomy of committees by stating that 'Cabinet Committees are meant to exercise fully the authority delegated them by Cabinet: *otherwise the point of establishing them would be lost*, the proper business of the Committees impeded and the Agenda of Cabinet itself unnecessarily cluttered' (New Zealand Cabinet Office, n.d., ch.D para. 3.3; emphasis added).

In Australia, according to the Secretary to the Department of the Prime Minister and Cabinet, 'The usual pattern has been that standing committees make final decisions, as do *ad hoc* committees if authorised by Cabinet to do so' (Yeend, 1979, 11). There are situations where a particular matter might come up again (e.g. in the context of the budget) or where a particular committee decision forms part of a group of interrelated decisions which for other reasons need to go to cabinet. In Australia it is accepted that in a minister wishing to have further consideration given to a particular matter in full cabinet could do so by raising the matter with the prime minister.

1.7 Cabinet

Just as cabinet committees perform a variety of functions, so full cabinets have a number of roles too, either potentially or in practice. These vary considerably in the extent to which the cabinet is initiating or reacting to events, and the extent to which it is concerned with an overview of government policies as a whole or largely self-contained issues.

One possible role for the full cabinet is the setting of strategic guidelines within which cabinet committees and individual ministers operate. This is, however, not a good description of the role of cabinets in practice, which tend not to deal with such guidelines, and in so far as there are general guidelines these emerge through political parties. The Heath government in Britain in the early 1970s attempted this role through six-monthly policy reviews, but from at least mid-1971 onwards cabinet reacted to events, rather than vice versa. Cabinet is largely a collection of departmental ministers rather than a collection of executives concerned with comprehensive strategic planning for the government as a whole. Only when the inevitable interdepartmental implications or political sensitivity of issues arise do ministers have to wrench themselves out of their departmental cocoon, and even then they may be more concerned with fighting for their departments' interests than a whole-government perspective, let alone a long-term one (see Seymour-Ure, 1971).

Another possible role for full cabinets is to review cabinet committee decisions selectively. Review of all but a few cabinet committee decisions is impracticable and where such a system theoretically operates, by far the majority of decisions are confirmed by cabinet without alterations. Where cabinet committee decisions are reviewable by full cabinet, one can expect a law of anticipated reactions to come into play. In arriving at decisions or recommendations to cabinet the committees would take into account the decision most likely to be acceptable to members of the full cabinet or, at a minimum, the one least likely to be challenged or altered. However, in cabinet systems like Britain, Australia and New Zealand matters resolved in cabinet committees cannot normally be reopened in full cabinet. In Britain they will not even be placed on the cabinet agenda. The full cabinet may simply not have the opportunity to reject or refer back or amend such decisions.

Full cabinets can act as court-of-appeal from cabinet committees. This role is explicitly recognized by Canada and New Zealand but constrained in Britain and Australia. Ministers have to operate self-denial in exercising any right-of-appeal, otherwise it may be counterproductive. The existence of a right-of-appeal, even if in largely token form (as in Britain) is an important safety valve, without which it might be difficult to secure consent to the effective decision-making of cabinet committees. Even where largely symbolic, the right-of-appeal role of the cabinet is important in maintaining the constitutional myth of collective cabinet decision-making and responsibility. There are cases, though relatively rare, where a strong minister in Britain can successfully press the prime minister to reopen an issue.

An important role for cabinets is as resolver of controversial issues that cabinet committees have been unable to resolve, or which go straight to cabinet. Such issues may not be the ones which are most significant on objective criteria such as the volume of resources committed to the issue but are more likely to be issues which are likely to be politically controversial or symbolic. This can refer either to disagreement within cabinet or anticipated reaction from the legislature, interest groups or the wider public. However, as chapter 4 on the United Kingdom shows, there is no guaranteed mechanism for ensuring that issues which may turn out to be controversial do in fact reach the full cabinet, or even a cabinet committee. The use of the 'political' rather than 'objective' criteria for setting the agenda of cabinet is typical of Britain and New Zealand and also applies to cabinets in other countries, with the important exception that where disagreement within a coalition government reflects cleavages between parties, attempted resolution is more likely to take place through inter-party mechanisms rather than in cabinet. The relative exclusion of issues which have large-scale resource implications or are otherwise important but are not politically controversial emphasizes the extent to which cabinet structures are designed to filter out as many issues as possible and establish political priorities for the cabinet's time.

A substantial proportion of the time of cabinet is taken up in receiving reports, including 'the gradual unfolding of events, especially abroad about which it can do little' (Jones, 1975: 33; see also Seymour-Ure, 1971: 202). This role may seem unimportant in decision-making terms, but it does have an important solitary function, giving an identifiable focus to what would otherwise be 'an amorphous group of about one hundred MPs forming the government' (Seymour-Ure, 1971: 202). Given that most actions of government are not taken by all ministers acting collectively, the fact that all cabinet ministers are collectively briefed about some decisions and matters of concern helps to reinforce the doctrine of collective responsibility in countries which subscribe to it.

Finally, cabinets perform a legitimating role, by their very existence as much as by what they actually discuss or decide. Because cabinet committee decisions are made in the name of the cabinet they may be regarded as having the same weight as decisions actually made in the cabinet. This applies whether the decision-

making role of the committee is formally recognized or not. Vinde
and Petri (1980:30) note that the main importance of the formal
weekly cabinet meetings in Sweden, which last less than half an
hour, is perhaps to 'constitute an expression of the Government's
collective responsibility for all decisions'. The daily luncheon
meetings, which Swedish cabinet ministers regularly attend, provide
a highly informal but strongly institutionalized arena for discussing
and resolving controversial issues.

1.8 Party
In coalition governments some decision-making necessarily involves
individuals belonging to more than one political party. Minority
government decision-making may also involve more than one party
because of the government's dependence upon other parties in the
legislature. These points are important because in the countries
considered here government by a single party with a parliamentary
majority has been the exception rather than the rule since 1945.
Only in Canada, Japan, New Zealand and the United Kingdom has
single-majority government been the norm. In continental Europe
the only lengthy periods of government by party with a parliamentary majority have been in Norway from 1945–61 and in Austria
1971–83. To state that decision-making involved ministers of more
than one party is not to say that it necessarily involves partisan
conflict. For instance, structural conflict between spending ministries and the ministry of finance are likely to occur, whether or not
the ministers involved are of the same or different parties. Coalition
governments will have a more or less institutionalized procedure for
resolving inter-party disputes, but for ministers to raise all disagreements to this level may be counterproductive.

Disputes between coalition partners may be referred to a cabinet
committee for resolution. The Estimates Committee in the first two
post-war Irish coalition governments seems to have served this
purpose, but mainly because there was no well-established cabinet
committee system so that disputes tended to go straight to cabinet
(Chubb, 1974: 145). Cabinet committees may also be deliberately
used as a means of resolving differences between parties before they
reach the party leadership. The newly established cabinet committee system in Denmark was used in this way during the 1978-9
Liberal-Socialist coalition government (see chapter 7 and Christensen, 1982: 13). Similarly, in Norway the establishment of a coalition
government after a long period of single-party rule led to the
creation of a whole series of permanent and ad hoc committees
(Solstad, 1969: 165). Previous Labour governments had not found a
formal system of cabinet committees necessary and the innovation

was not continued when Labour returned to office.

The site of inter-party negotiations may be a more or less institutionalized grouping of political leaders quite outside the normal cabinet committee framework. Good examples from West Germany are the so-called Kressbonner circle during the CDU-SPD Grand Coalition government from 1966 to 1969 and the Schaumburger Runde weekly luncheon meeting of SPD and FDP leaders, both of which made binding agreements which were subsequently simply ratified by the cabinet and identified areas on which agreement could not be reached.

The most institutionalized example of this process is the Coalition Committee operated during the nineteen years of the Socialist-Peoples Party Grand Coalition in Austria, before it came to an end in 1966. The membership and responsibilities of this committee were agreed between the coalition partners at the beginning of each new parliament as part of a broad coalition pact. Significantly, membership of the committee was not limited to cabinet ministers. It included the general secretaries of the parties, the leaders of the party groups in parliament and the main party-linked interest groups. In 1962 only four of the twelve members of the committee were also members of the cabinet (Steiner, 1972: 254). The cabinet was merely a rubber-stamp for the decisions made in the committee.

Coalition governments may also create means for monitoring the activities of individual ministers by coalition partners. The appointment of deputy ministers from a party other than that of the responsible ministers is a typical device, employed, for example, in the Austrian Grand Coalition and in Italy. Such a system may increase the possibility that differences could be interpreted as inter-party ones. But it is worth noting that such monitoring systems are by no means universal; for example, they were not employed in the 1965–9 'bourgeois' coalition in Norway (Solstad, 1969: 164). Even in the case of Austria, where the role of deputy ministers as spies 'of one party implanted in a ministry administered by another party' is well-attested (Engelmann, 1966: 270), it is worth noting that during the nineteen years of two-party coalition the proportion of cabinet ministers supported by 'spies' provided by the coalition partner was never more than half (calculated from Gerlich, Ross and Stiefbold, 1968: D195–203). The key Finance Ministry, always a Peoples Party preserve, never had a Socialist deputy minister.

Intra-party negotiations, whether involving linkages with the parliamentary group or the extra-parliamentary organization, are another aspect of the role of party in decision-making. Such negotiations can exist in either single-party or coalition governments. The importance of this relationship will vary from country to country and between different types of party. An extreme case where both political norms and formal rules legitimate an important role for the party outside government concerns both National and Labour governments in New Zealand and Labor governments in Australia. All bills in New Zealand are submitted to the parliamentary caucus prior to introduction, whether or not they have cabinet approval. In Australia when Labor is in office all bills and regulations are submitted to the parliamentary caucus before submission to parliament. Under the Whitlam government from 1972 to 1975 measures were also submitted to caucus committees and committee members were given access to ministers and some civil servants (Crisp, 1973: 394). But is worth noting the limitations of such a link even in such propitious circumstances. Caucus consultations did not take place when parliament was not sitting and caucus involvement was 'irregular and unpredictable' (Smith, 1976: 202). The example of the MX missile decision taken in 1983 without caucus knowledge let alone involvement was referred to in 1.5, though left-wing dissatisfaction subsequently led to reversal of the decision, but again without caucus discussion.

The influence of parties which provide parliamentary support for minority governments but do not participate in the cabinet tends to be ad hoc in character. Support for a minority government may involve a commitment in terms of particular policies but does not involve the support parties in the normal decision-making processes of government. The period of the Lib-Lab pact in Britain between the Labour government and the small Liberal party from March 1977 to May 1978 is a case in point (see 4.4). In the Republic of Ireland, the bargain between Fianna Fail leader Charles Haughey and the independent Dublin representative Tony Gregory in March 1982, which gave Haughey a short-lived majority in the Dail at the price of written commitments totalling more than £100 million, does not seem to have involved Gregory's participation in the machinery of central government (see *Financial Times*, 10 March 1982).

Even in multi-party coalitions, the bulk of government decisions will not take the form of inter-party disputes and therefore will be handled through the decision arenas described above. The existence of a multiplicity of parties in government provides an additional cleavage around which disagreements may be formed, and may also result in the establishment of special party mechanisms for resolution of such disagreements. They should be seen as an addition to the other decision arenas rather than a substitue for any one of them.

References

Barnett, J. (1982) *Inside the Treasury*. London: Andre Deutsch.

Blondel, J. (1982) *The Organization of Governments: A Comparative Analysis of Governmental Structures*. London and Beverly Hills: Sage.

Castle, B. (1980) *The Castle Diaries 1974–6*. London: Weidenfeld and Nicolson.

Christensen, J.G. (1982) 'Growth by Exception: or the Vain Attempt to Impose Resource Scarcity on the Danish Public Sector', *Journal of Public Policy*, 2: 117–44.

Chubb, B. (1974) *Cabinet Government in Ireland*. Dublin: Institute of Public Administration.

Crisp, L.F. (1973) *Australian National Government*. Melbourne: Longman Cheshire.

Crossman, R. (1975, 1976, 1977) *The Diaries of a Cabinet Minister*, vols. 1–3. London: Hamish Hamilton and Jonathan Cape.

Engelmann, F. (1966) 'Austria: the Pooling of Opposition', in R.A. Dahl (ed.), *Political Opposition in Western Democracies*. New Haven: Yale University Press.

Gallagher, M. (1980) 'The Composition of Government in the Republic of Ireland, 1959–1980'. Paper presented to the European Consortium for Political Research Workshop on the Composition of Governments in Parliamentary Regimes, Florence, March 1980.

Gerlich, P., G. Ross and R. Stiefbold (eds) (1968) *Österreichisches Wahlhandbuch*. Vienna: Verlag für Jugund und Volk.

Jones, G. (1975) 'Development of the Cabinet', in W. Thornhill (ed.), *The Modernization of British Government*. London: Pitman.

Kaufman, G. (1981) *How to be a Minister*. London: Sidgwick and Jackson.

New Zealand Cabinet Office (n.d.) *New Zealand Cabinet Office Manual*. Wellington: New Zealand Cabinet Office.

Olsen, J. (1980) 'Governing Norway: Segmentation, Anticipation and Consensus Formation', in R. Rose and E. Suleiman (eds), *Presidents and Prime Ministers*. Washington DC: American Enterprise Institute.

Rose, R. (1980) 'Government against Sub-governments: a European Perspective', pp. 284–347 in R. Rose and E. Suleiman (eds), *Presidents and Prime Ministers*. Washington DC: American Enterprise Institute.

Rose, R. and E. Suleiman (eds) (1980) *Presidents and Prime Ministers*. Washington DC: American Enterprise Institute.

Seymour-Ure, C. (1971) 'The Disintegration of the Cabinet and the Neglected Issue of Cabinet Reform', *Parliamentary Affairs*, 24: 196–207.

Smith, R.F.I. (1976) 'Australian Cabinet Structures and Procedures', Appendix 4 in *Report of Royal Commission on Australian Government Administration*.

Solstad, A. (1969) 'The Norwegian Coalition System', *Scandinavian Political Studies*, 4.

Steiner, K. (1972) *Politics in Austria*. Boston: Little, Brown.

Vinde, P. and G. Petri (1978) *Swedish Government Administration*. Stockholm: Swedish Institute.

Walker, P. Gordon (1972) *The Cabinet*, revised edn. Glasgow and London: Fontana and Collins.

Wilson, H. (1971) *The Labour Government 1964–1970*. London: Weidenfeld and Nicolson and Michael Joseph.

Yeend, G. (1979) 'The Department of the Prime Minister and Cabinet in Perspective'. Address to the Australian Capital Territory Branch of the Royal Australian Institute of Public Administration.

2
Formal committee structures

Thomas T. Mackie and Brian W. Hogwood

2.1 Introduction

In this chapter we provide an overview of cabinet committee structures in the nineteen industrialized countries which have an unbroken record of parliamentary government since 1960 and which have political executives that are cabinet systems, having as head of government a prime minister who regularly chairs a meeting of ministers which has the formal authority to make or approve decisions on behalf of the government as a whole. Thus we do not include all countries which have some body called a cabinet (or council of ministers). The federal government in the United States of America, for example, has a cabinet but is clearly not a cabinet system and so is not covered here, since our purpose is to illuminate variations in cabinet systems. To avoid the need for continual special treatment, we have also excluded from consideration here the special hybrid form of government in France. These decision rules restrict our analysis to nineteen countries: Australia, Austria, Belgium, Canada, Denmark, Finland, Iceland, Ireland, Israel, Italy, Japan, Luxembourg, the Netherlands, New Zealand, Norway, Sweden, Switzerland, the United Kingdom and West Germany.

2.2 Which countries have cabinet committees?

Cabinet committees are found in sixteen of the nineteen countries examined in this chapter (see Table 2.1). The exceptions are Iceland, Luxembourg and Sweden. This obliges us to confront the problem of the 'dogs that did not bark in the night-time'. For readers who are unfamiliar with Sir Arthur Conan Doyle's classic detective stories based on the character Sherlock Holmes, the following is the relevant passage from *Silver Blaze:*

> 'Is there any other point to which you would wish to draw my attention?'
> 'To the curious incident of the dog in the night-time.'
> 'The dog did nothing in the night-time.'
> 'That was the curious incident', remarked Sherlock Holmes.

In other words, if we are to establish the importance of cabinet committees, we have to try to explain why some countries do not have them and perhaps to show that they do have functional equivalents.

One possible explanation might be the size of the government. The smaller the number of ministers the greater the likelihood that completely informal procedures may operate which will include all ministers concerned. Size does have some influence on the existence of cabinet committees (see Table 2.1). Two of the countries with much smaller than average number of ministers, Iceland and Luxembourg, do not operate cabinet committees. But Switzerland, with only seven ministers, does, and Sweden, with nineteen ministers, very close to the average number, does not.

The countries included in this study vary considerably both in the absolute size and the relative scope of activity undertaken by government (see Table 2.2). With populations ranging from 118,000,000 to 200,000 the amount of government activity will inevitably vary enormously. Iceland and Luxembourg are clearly exceptional in terms of their tiny population, small number of cabinet ministers and low *absolute* level of public expenditure. For these reasons, ministers may more easily operate a highly informal decision-making system.

Sweden does not fit this pattern. One plausible explanation for this exception is the stability of party control in Sweden. The Social Democrats were in office continuously from 1934 until 1976 and have been in government again since 1982, though as part of a national coalition during the Second World War and in coalition with the Agrarian Party from 1951 to 1957. Even more striking is the stability of office holding. Herman's (1975) analysis of seventeen Western countries shows that during the period from 1945 to 1971 the average duration in office of the Swedish cabinet minister was seventy-one months, twenty months longer than the next most stable country, Iceland. The experience of governing over a lengthy period of time by a single party and by a relatively stable group of ministers may allow particularly informal methods of joint decision-making to develop. The well-attested example of such a process is the daily luncheon meetings of the Swedish cabinet (Vinde and Petri, 1978: 30).

2.3 The number and functions of committees

2.3.1 *The number and types of committees*
The available data for the number of cabinet committees are incomplete, but from the information we have for eleven countries

TABLE 2.1
Cabinet committees and cabinet ministers

Country	Cabinet committees in operation	No. of ministers*		
		In cabinet	Not in cabinet	Total
Australia	Yes	17	10	27
Austria	Yes	15	8	23
Belgium	Yes	15	10	25
Canada	Yes	40	—	40
Denmark	Yes	21	—	21
Finland	Yes	17	—	17
Germany	Yes	17	5	22
Iceland	No	10	—	10
Ireland	Yes	15	15	30
Israel	Yes	25	6	31
Italy	Yes	30	58	88
Japan	Yes	13	9	22
Luxembourg	No	12	—	12
Netherlands	Yes	14	16	30
New Zealand	Yes	21	—	18
Norway	Yes	18	—	18
Sweden	No	19	—	19
Switzerland	Yes	7	—	7
United Kingdom	Yes	19	27	46
Average		18		27

Note: * Membership of government after most recent general election.
Source: *Keesing's Contemporary Archives*, vol. XXVIII (1982)-vol. XXXI (1985).

we can see that for similarly sized cabinets the number of committees varies considerably (see Table 2.3). The clear outlier is the United Kingdom with more than twice as many committees (including subcommittees and ad hoc committees) as any other country. As the record of British cabinet committees is incomplete the actual difference is certainly greater. The number of committees bears no relationship to the size of the cabinet or to the number of ministers in the government as a whole. The British cabinet formed after the 1983 election comprised nineteen ministers and there were twenty-seven ministers (not including parliamentary secretaries) not in the cabinet, but the Canadian cabinet formed in September 1984 with forty ministers manages with only ten committees. At the other

TABLE 2.2
Scale and scope of activity of government

Country	Population (m)	Govt. expenditure $(US)bn	Govt. expenditure as % of GDP
Australia	15.2	46.8	31.1
Austria	7.6	29.7	44.0
Belgium	9.9	43.4	53.3
Canada	24.7	138.0	42.2
Denmark	5.1	31.8	56.7
Finland	4.8	17.8	37.3
Germany	61.6	294.6	44.8
Iceland	0.2	0.6	27.6
Ireland	3.5	8.5	48.3
Israel	4.1	n.a.	n.a.
Italy	56.6	172.2	48.5
Japan	118.4	306.6	26.5
Luxembourg	0.4	1.5	45.7
Netherlands	14.3	77.7	58.3
New Zealand	3.2	n.a.	n.a.
Norway	4.1	25.0	45.5
Sweden	8.3	55.2	60.3
Switzerland	6.5	27.6	28.1
United Kingdom	56.3	200.3	44.6

Source: OECD *Observer*, no. 127, March 1984: 20–4.

TABLE 2.3
Size of cabinet and numbers of cabinet committees

Country	Size of cabinet	No. of committees
Australia	17	10
Belgium	15	7
Canada	40	10
Denmark	21	14
Finland	17	3
Germany	17	16
Japan	13	10
Netherlands	14	14
New Zealand	18	9
Switzerland	7	12
United Kingdom	19	38*

Note: * Known ministerial committees, including subcommittees.
Sources: As for Table 2.1; Table 4.2, chapter 4; sources acknowledged in preface.

end of the scale the seven member Swiss Bundesrat operates twelve cabinet committees (see chapter 9).

There is some variation in the number of committees over time as well as between countries. These changes do not necessarily represent a secular increase in the number of committees. In Denmark, for instance, the number of committees increased from eleven in 1971 to twenty-five ten years later, but the present four-party coalition government which came into office in 1982 reduced the number to fourteen (see 7.4.1). The incumbent governments in Australia, New Zealand, Canada and Belgium have all reduced the number of cabinet committees. In the Netherlands and Switzerland the number of committees has moved in an upward direction (see chapters 8 and 9).

2.3.2 *The functional distribution of committees*

Dealing first with such elements of uniformity as exist, all the countries for which we have information have at least one committee dealing with foreign affairs and/or defence. All countries have a committee dealing with economic policy, and all but two (Netherlands and Japan) have a committee dealing with budget or finance policy. The fact that in the Netherlands budgetary questions are dealt with either bilaterally between the finance ministry and the spending department or in the cabinet as a whole is a clear indication of the limited policy-making role of cabinet committees (see 8.4). At the other extreme, none of the countries has a separate committee for health.

Only Germany and Switzerland have a separate agriculture committee. The central importance of agricultural policy in European Community countries means that agricultural matters nearly always have important external policy implications and such questions are presumably normally dealt with in foreign or European policy committees.

It is worth noting that in all four countries with a Westminster-style parliamentary system committees with responsibility for managing legislation have been established. Although in all these countries the parliamentary stage of the legislative process is of relatively minor importance substantively, the symbolic importance of parliament is very considerable and the number of days devoted to plenary sittings is very much higher than in other parliamentary systems. In the early 1970s, for instance, the four Westminster-style parliaments sat for an average of 945 hours a year whilst the other parliaments sat for an average of only 262 hours (calculated from Inter-Parliamentary Union, 1976: 298–311). Managing the parliamentary timetable is an essential part of government business.

2.4 The establishment and composition of committees

2.4.1 *How decisions to establish committees are made*

In most countries for which information is available cabinet committees are established on an informal basis. Even when the membership of committees is routinely made public by the government of the day most committees have no statutory character. There are exceptions to this rule. In Canada the Treasury Board, created in 1967, is a committee of the Privy Council established by statute. In Belgium the membership and remit of committees are established by an *arrêté royal*. In the Netherlands members of committees set up under the standing orders of the Council of Ministers are published in the annual state calendar. In Commonwealth countries the primary role in the establishment of cabinet committees is played by the prime minister. In Canada and New Zealand and probably in Australia and the United Kingdom the cabinet secretariat will routinely provide incoming governments with proposals for membership of committees that already exist, but initiative for the establishment of new committees and further remits lies with the head of government. In New Zealand the prime minister's nominations are subject to ratification by the cabinet, which sometimes alters them.

In continental European countries where coalition governments are the norm the situation is less clear. In Switzerland the initiative for the establishment of a committee usually comes from the minister heading the department most concerned, who ends up chairing the committee (see 9.3.2). However, Switzerland is probably an extreme case in that the Federal Council is a genuinely collegial body whose chair, the President of the Confederation, rotates on an annual basis among its members. But in all countries with coalition governments the role of the prime minister will depend on the relative political weight of the coalition partners, even if the prime minister is formally responsible for the creation of cabinet committees.

2.4.2 *How committee chairmen are appointed*

In any committee system the role of the chairman is an important one. Hence the question of who becomes chairman is worth investigating. Three general alternatives seem to be operated in the appointment of chairmen. Firstly, the minister most affected by the work of a committee will be appointed chairman. This is always the case in Switzerland and Denmark.

Secondly, the prime minister will chair all or virtually all committees; this may, however, be a formality, with the actual practice varying under different prime ministers. This is the case in Belgium and the Netherlands and has occasionally been the case elsewhere. For example, Weller notes in chapter 6 that in the Hawke government in Australia most cabinet committee meetings are chaired by the prime minister.

Thirdly, the prime minister may chair only a few committees which he or she regards as having particular political weight or sensitivity. Clearly this would include inner-cabinet-like committees such as Priorities and Planning in Canada. Committees dealing with security and intelligence matters are similarly chaired by the head of government.

The appointment of the committee chairman is particularly important in the British system given the lack of formal votes and the key role of the chairman in summing up the decision of the committee (see 4.3).

2.4.3 *How the composition of committees is determined*
The two main criteria which may affect appointment to committees are functional and representational. Since one of the principal purposes of the establishment of such committees is to solve differences between departments with overlapping jurisdictions, functional criteria are bound to play a primary role in the allocation of committee assignments. In this context the most interesting political question may be which minister is *not*. For instance, Kellas (1975: 46) notes the absence of the Secretary of State for Scotland from the key Economic Policy Committee during the 1964–70 Labour government in the United Kingdom.

Representational interests may affect the composition of a committee in several ways. In many countries the need to ensure adequate representation of linguistic, religious and territorial interests is a paramount factor in cabinet making. In a coalition government, all the coalition partners will demand at least proportional representation within the cabinet (Franklin and Browne, 1973). Are similar considerations apparent in the establishment of cabinet committees or are they confined to the more highly visible (and perhaps largely symbolic) area of the government as a whole?

In Canada the balance of regional interests between Ontario, Quebec, the Maritime and Western provinces is very important. In cabinet representation from all major regions is essential. For governments whose support is regionally imbalanced prime ministers have resorted to appointments from the nominated Senate. For instance, the 1980–4 Trudeau government's supporters in the House of Commons contained only two MPs from the Western provinces

TABLE 2.4
Canada: regional distribution of Liberal MPs, cabinet ministers and cabinet committee members, July 1980

	Quebec	Ontario	Maritime Provinces	Western Provinces	Total
MPs	74 (50.3%)	52 (35.4%)	19 (12.9%)	2 (1.4%)	147
Cabinet ministers	12 (36.4%)	12 (36.4%)	5 (15.2%)	4 (12.1%)	33
Cabinet Committees					
Priorities and Planning	5	3	2	2	12
Treasury Board	2	1	2	1	6
Legislation and House Planning	5	3	0	1	9
Communications	3	3	2	2	10
Economic Development	5	5	4	3	17
Foreign and Defence Policy	5	6	2	2	15
Government Operations	4	3	2	1	10
Labour Relations	5	4	2	1	12
Public Service	3	2	1	0	6
Security and Intelligence	4	2	1	1	8
Social Development	4	5	3	1	13
Special Committee of Council	3	4	2	1	10
Western Affairs	2	5	1	4	12

Source: Simpson (1981); membership of the cabinet committees published by the Prime Minister's Office, 10 July 1981.

(see Table 2.4). One of these became a cabinet minister as did three senators. As a standard procedure Privy Council Office staff take into account the need for regional representation in drawing up proposals to the prime minister for the composition of committees. The primary criterion employed is functional, but committees are routinely 'topped up' with ministers whose functional responsibilities are hardly relevant to the committee's remit in order to ensure representation of all regions. In particular, in the last few governments all regions have been represented in the government's 'inner cabinet' (so called during the 1980 Clark government and otherwise styled the Priorities and Planning Committee) however minuscule the numbers or modest in political weight the regional MPs were (see 5.8).

In Belgium the importance of language is such that since 1970 it has been a constitutional requirement that the membership of the cabinet be equally divided between members of the French-speaking and Dutch-speaking communities. An examination of the committees established from 1972 to 1981 reveals the importance of representative as well as functional imperatives (Van Hassel, 1981). The presence of the prime minister and the deputy prime ministers on almost every committee ensured the inclusion of the leaders of the parties comprising the government. As in Canada, committees were sometimes topped up with ministers whose functional responsibilities were hardly relevant to the committee's remit in order to ensure representational balance between the parties and the two linguistic communities.

In Australia, Aitkin and Jinks (1980: 85) note that cabinet portfolios are usually allocated roughly in proportion to the number of members of the House of Representatives from the various states: 'It is politically desirable to have the smallest states represented by at least one minister although perhaps in a junior office'. Liberal-National Party coalitions introduce the possibility of party criteria also, but functional rather than representative criteria seem to predominate. Weller notes that one reason for the inclusion of Peter Nixon, the National Party Minister of Primary Industry, in the important Foreign Affairs and Monetary Committees was 'as a means of ensuring coalition balance on the committees' (see 6.2.3).

The New Zealand cabinet normally includes at least a couple of South Island ministers of reasonable seniority. The Auckland region, where the bulk of the population lives, must not be seen to obtrude too much. There is also a need to have a strong representation of ministers with a farming background. National Party cabinets are chosen by the prime minister. Labour prime ministers, who have been in office for only six of the last thirty-five years, receive from the parliamentary caucus a list of names to whom they allocate portfolios. The allocation of committee memberships relates more often than not to portfolio responsibilities. Indeed, the Cabinet Office usually supplies the prime minister with an initial list allocating portfolios among the committees on the basis of the relevance of the activity.

In the Netherlands, where coalition government is the norm, party criteria may *prima facie* be important. Chapter 8 demonstrates that this is indeed the case. Functional criteria may determine the composition of cabinet committees but the need for all the coalition partners to be represented on major committees is itself one of the factors which are taken into account when the initial allocation of government portfolios is being decided during the cabinet formation process (see 8.5).

In Denmark cabinet committee membership has been used to compensate minor coalition partners who have been unable to secure a major ministerial portfolio and to compensate a major party for the loss of an important ministry (see 7.4.2).

In Switzerland linguistic as well as partisan criteria could in principle be important in a country with three major languages and a four-party government which has been in office for more than forty years, but with committees of only three members representational equity is arithmetically impossible (see 9.3.3). In the overwhelming majority of cases functional criteria determine committee membership. Only in a few very politically sensitive areas have party and linguistic considerations had any effect, and then only on one of the three committee members (see 9.5).

In the United Kingdom, the primacy of functional criteria in the allocation of committee responsibilities does not preclude the possibility of 'packing' or 'rigging' a committee, particularly where committee appointments are a prime ministerial prerogative. This can occur whether through the appointment of the chairman or through ensuring an ideological bias in committee membership (while still meeting functional and other criteria). More generally, the prime minister can determine the composition of the committee both directly and through the allocation of ministerial portfolios. The prime minister can even disband a committee and reconstitute it to exclude ministers who took a line opposed to that of the prime minister or other members of the committee concerned (see 4.3).

Overall, party, regional or language criteria do not overshadow functional criteria for the allocation of committee responsibilities. Representative criteria may be important in the overall composition of a cabinet and in the allocation of particular portfolios and this may have indirect effect upon the cabinet committee assignments. The addition of members to committees in order to ensure adequate partisan, regional or language representation is the main way in which such factors affect committee composition.

2.5 Civil servants and cabinet government

The role of civil servants in cabinet government is obviously complex. The constitutional distinction between elected ministers as the formulators of policy and appointed civil servants as the passive executants of their wishes has been universally recognized as a largely false one. But, as Aberbach, Putnam and Rockman (1981) have convincingly demonstrated, the extent and character of the linkages between civil servants and other political actors varies considerably from one polity to another. This section considers those relationships in the context of the cabinet committee system. The role of civil servants as members of cabinet committees, the role of committees of civil servants paralleling ministerial committees and the role of cabinet secretariats in servicing cabinet committees will be briefly considered in turn.

2.5.1 *Civil service membership of cabinet committees*
The participation of civil servants in committees varies widely between countries and to some extent within countries. At one extreme in the Netherlands civil servants are *officially* members of twelve out of fourteen cabinet committees. The civil servants involved are mostly directors-general of government departments, but other important officials are also included. For instance, the Director of the Central Bank is a member of the Finance Committee and the Netherlands Permanent Representative at the NATO Council is a member of the General Defence Council (Secretariat of the Civil Service Department, 1982). In Canada the practice of civil servants standing in for their ministers, even though they are not formally members of the committee, is a common one (Campbell and Szablowski, 1979: 155–7).

In several countries most committees function without the participation of civil servants but a few committees do include them. These committees tend to be of considerable importance. For instance, Christensen describes the role of Danish civil servants in the Coordination Committee and the Public Sector Modernization Committee (which is responsible for budgetary policy) in Denmark (see 7.5).

Weller notes the involvement of civil servants in the Cabinet Economic Committee in New Zealand (see 6.3.2). In Australia Smith notes that civil servants sometimes attended meetings of the ad hoc Expenditure Review Committee which played an important role in the Whitlam government (1972–5). However, this was rather exceptional: in Australia, except during the Chiffley government (1945–9) when civil servants were routinely included in committees, a rigid separation between civil servants and minister has prevailed. In Belgium a similar barrier appears to be the norm.

The presence of civil servants in committees must be distinguished from the form their participation takes. Because of the secrecy surrounding the deliberations of cabinet committees, even in those countries where committee membership is well-documented, it is very difficult to draw even a very partial picture. It might be reasonable to assume that in governments where ministers themselves are frequently civil servants rather than members of parliament, such as the Netherlands civil service, committee members would feel particularly uninhibited, but this view is necessarily speculative.

In Commonwealth countries the convention is that civil servants attend committees only to record discussion, or at most to provide points of information on request. In general, the role of civil servants in Australia and New Zealand seems to reflect this convention. In New Zealand Galvin (1982: 29) notes that in the Cabinet Economic Committee 'the direct relationship between a Minister and his Permanent Head became blurred' and that Permanent Heads were able to put forward their own rather than their ministers' viewpoints (see 6.3.2). However, Smith (1976: 196) notes that in Australia civil servants who attended the Expenditure Review Committee rarely took part in general discussion.

In Canada and the United Kingdom the role of civil servants is more expansive, with the former country differing most drastically from the conventional picture. One of the few empirical studies of the participation of civil servants in mixed committees is Campbell (1983). His study of top civil servants in Washington, Ottawa and London is relevant in this context for what he can tell us about British and Canadian mandarins. A clear distinction between the two emerges. Far more of his sample of Canadian civil servants attend committees regularly than their British counterparts: 45 per cent compared to 15 per cent. More importantly, the Canadians are much more likely to participate actively in committee rather than to act as observers. In terms of involvement and participation of civil servants, then, Canada is clearly different in degree if not in kind from the other Commonwealth countries.

2.5.2 *Civil service committees paralleling ministerial committees*
Civil service committees which parallel ministerial committees should be clearly distinguished from the vast network of interdepartmental committees which are a characteristic and important feature of the decision-making structure of Western governments. The importance of such interdepartmental committees, especially as they link government with interest groups, is pointed to in several of the country studies in this book. The concern here, however, is with those civil service committees which are specifically linked to ministerial committees.

The British practice of a three-tier system of cabinet, ministerial and official committees is, not surprisingly, to be observed in other Commonwealth countries. In Australia and Canada the system seems to have been the norm since the Second World War, despite considerable changes in ministerial committee structures. In New Zealand the system seems less well-developed; the Cabinet Manual records that only three of the thirteeen ministerial committees operating during the Muldoon government were served by committees of officials. Admittedly, this included the important Cabinet Economic Committee.

In Denmark a network of parallel committees was not set up until 1977. The system was modelled on the civil service committee which had worked very successfully with the ministerial committee on European Community Affairs during the previous five years (see 7.5). The Netherlands and Swiss cabinet systems seem to operate without any parallel committees. In Belgium, on the other hand, ministerial committees are routinely served by civil service committees (Van Hassel, 1983: 36).

The patterns described above reflect the formal institutional framework. The importance of civil service committees in the cabinet process cannot be directly inferred from such information any more than the role of civil servants in mixed committees can be adduced simply from knowing that they belong to such committees. Again, Campbell's (1983) study of central agencies in Britain, Canada and the United States provides a clue both as to why civil service committees are set up in the first place and how they operate. Campbell describes how Canadian civil servants de-emphasize roles on interdepartmental committees compared to their British counterparts. Senior British civil servants are far more likely to perceive such committee work as crucial. Over 90 per cent of British respondents saw such committees (covering both civil service cabinet committees and other interdepartmental committees of civil servants) as effective as opposed to only half of the Canadians (Campbell, 1983: 281). Where civil servants are routinely involved in shared decision-making with ministers in mixed committees, interdepartmental committees are likely to be downgraded in importance. Where the barriers to joint involvement are higher, as in Australia, Belgium and New Zealand, the incentives for the establishment of effective parallel committees of civil servants may be higher.

2.5.3 *Cabinet secretariats*
The role of cabinet secretariats in the operations of cabinet committees varies considerably. In countries where cabinet secretariats have been well-established for many years they provide at least the secretarial support for individual ministerial and interdepartmental committees. This is the case in the Commonwealth countries, Belgium and the Netherlands. While some secretariats, such as the Cabinet Office in London and above all the Privy Council Office in Ottawa, have a high profile others, like the New Zealand Office, are 'essentially a processing and secretarial unit' (see 6.3.2).

In countries where the cabinet secretariat has only developed recently even this procedural task may be beyond its capabilities. In

Denmark, for instance, this task is carried out by officials from the department whose minister presides over the committees and not by a central body.

2.6 Conclusion

Our overview of cabinet structures in Western parliamentary systems has shown that cabinet committees are a usual but by no means ubiquitous phenomenon. They do not exist in the smallest countries and in others they are either non-existent or their role is very modest. In those countries which do have committees (and which are adequately documented) the number of extant committees varies considerably. The use of committees has spread considerably in the post-1945 period and especially in the late 1960s and early 1970s. There is no relationship between the size of the cabinet or of the ministry as a whole and the number of committees in operation at any one time.

In some countries, certainly in the Commonwealth, the role of the prime minister in setting up committees and deciding their remit is crucial. In continental countries the role of the prime minister is less clear cut.

Functional criteria are the overwhelmingly important grounds for the selection of members of committees and thus committee members to a considerable extent select themselves. However, two caveats should be mentioned. In countries where regional or linguistic differences are important and cabinet committees are well-developed representational factors are also important. In coalition governments the need for representation of coalition partners is itself functional for the maintenance of government.

Mixed committees of civil servants are very important in Canada and the Netherlands. In other countries most committees exclude civil servants from active participation but even in these cases a few, usually very important, committees are mixed in character, and in these civil servants sometimes play an active role. The network of parallel committees of civil servants is a central feature of Commonwealth countries, though less so in New Zealand than in the others. This system appears to be less common in continental European countries, with the exception of Belgium. In all cases wide networks of official committees outside the cabinet system are a very important part of the framework of decision-making.

Cabinet committees are, therefore, widespread, but the importance of cabinet committees as a decision-making arena in government varies very considerably.

References

Aberbach, J., R. Putnam and B. Rockman (1981) *Bureaucrats and Politicians in Western Democracies*. Cambridge, Mass.: Harvard University Press.

Aitkin, D. and Jinks, B. (1980) *Australian Political Institutions*. Carlton, Victoria: Pitman Australia.

Campbell, C. (1983) *Governments under Stress: Political Executives and Key Bureaucrats in Washington, London and Ottawa*. Toronto: University of Toronto Press.

Campbell, C. and G. Szablowski (1979) *The Superbureaucrats: Structure and Behaviour in Central Agencies*. Toronto: Macmillan.

Franklin, M. and E. Browne (1973) 'Aspects of Coalition Payoffs in European Parliamentary Democracies', *American Political Science Review*, 67: 453–69.

Galvin, B.V.J. (1982) 'Some Reflections on the Operation of the Executive'. Paper presented to the New Zealand Political Studies Association Conference, 18 May 1982.

Herman, V. (1975) 'Comparative Perspectives on Ministerial Stability in Britain', in V. Herman and J. Alt (eds), *Cabinet Studies: A Reader*. London: Macmillan.

Inter-Parliamentary Union (1976) *Parliaments of the World*. Compiled by V. Herman with F. Mendel. London: Macmillan.

Kellas, J. (1975) *The Scottish Political System*, 2nd edn. Cambridge: Cambridge University Press.

Secretariat of the Civil Service Department, Ministry of General Affairs (1982) *Overzicht van onderraden en de darbij behorende Inderdeparmentale Voorbereidingscommissies ambtelijke voorportalen*.

Simpson, K. (ed.) (1981) *Canadian Who's Who, 1981*. Toronto: Toronto University Press.

Smith, R. (1976) 'Australian Cabinet Structures and Procedures', in *Report of the Royal Commission on Australian Administration*, Appendix 4.G: 190–211.

Van Hassel, H. (1981) 'Organising Belgian Cabinets: Governments in a Turmoil', *Res Publica*, 23: 277–306.

Van Hassel, H. (1983) 'Cabinet committees in Belgium'. Paper presented to the European Consortium for Political Research Workshop on Cabinet Committees in Comparative Perspective, Freiburg, West Germany, 20–5 March 1983.

Vinde, P. and G. Petri (1978) *Swedish Government Administration*, 2nd revised edn. Stockholm: Swedish Institute.

3
Cabinet committees in context

Thomas T. Mackie and Brian W. Hogwood

Chapters 1 and 2 have shown that there is a variety of arrangement for decision-making ranging from individual ministers acting as heads of their own departments to the full cabinet meeting and acting collectively. Of these arrangements cabinet committees play an important role in most countries, a role which has received formal recognition in a number of them. While prime ministers can play an important role in many (but not all) of the countries operating cabinet systems (in terms of determining what committees shall operate, their composition and their chairmanship) and may chair many key committees, our focus on cabinet committees as one of a number of decision-making arenas in cabinet systems helps to balance the perspective gained from simply looking at the 'power of the prime minister'.

No clear-cut model of cabinet structure emerges from our study, either in terms of the role of cabinet committees or the broader pattern of executive decision-making. What we can say is that a simple hierarchical model of executive decision-making is inappropriate. First of all, the idea of a hierarchical pyramid of individual ministers topped by cabinet committees, topped by cabinet, topped by the prime minister, with implied delegation downwards and upwards referral of all strategic or important decisions is not convincing. In many countries, authority for political decision-making affecting single departments resides in the individual minister and not in collective responsibility of the cabinet. Indeed, this principle is sometimes constitutionally recognized, for instance in the *Ressortprinzip* of Article 65 of the German Basic Law (see Ridley, 1966; Mayntz, 1980: 143).

However, even in countries with the doctrine of collective ministerial responsibility, we find individual ministers exercising a wide power of decision-making about their departments, with *the minister* exercising much discretion about which issues should be referred to colleagues. Where an issue is of such a nature that it does not just affect his own department, it is more likely to be resolved by interministerial negotiation or cabinet committee decision than by full cabinet. A number of decisions will be taken in full cabinet, but these will not necessarily include all the most important ones, unless one accepts the circular definition that politically important decisions are those which are taken in cabinet. The prime minister will rarely be directly involved in issues, though he or she will be able to select a very limited number of issues for personal intervention and that intervention will often be decisive. The prime minister will often be unaware of decisions taken in the name of his or her government, even decisions taken in the name of his or her government, even decisions taken in the name of cabinet committees (though the Cabinet Office or equivalent would draw his or her attention to anything considered to be of importance). The prime minister's role in such decisions is to shape the decision-making process in some countries by deciding on the number, coverage, composition and chairmanship of committees as well as which ones to chair personally.

Thus in examining how decision-making takes place within cabinet structures it is essential that we do not confine analysis to the process by which individual decisions are made (whether case studies or a broad sample of decisions) since the interplay of power and personalities takes place in a context which has itself been structured to shape the range of likely outcomes, even if the Prime Minister or other key actors do not necessarily intervene in the discussion of an issue.

The model of cabinet structure which best describes most cabinet systems is one of interrelated but fragmented decision arenas derived from membership of a cabinet which gives the system a focus but which itself takes only a small proportion of decisions in full session. This is not inconsistent with the fact that cabinets normally have a full agenda of issues for decision; it is to prevent overcrowding of the cabinet agenda that mechanisms for taking decisions elsewhere are established. Cabinet committees or their informal equivalents perform a crucial role in making these systems workable. This picture of a fragmented set of overlapping decision arenas rather than a neat hierarchical arrangement is similar to the picture of the 'disintegration' of the British cabinet painted by Seymour-Ure (1971). However, we prefer not to use the word disintegration, with its connotation of a process of movement away from an integrated cabinet, so as to avoid the implication that in all countries there used to be a 'golden age' of cabinet government in which the cabinet members sitting collectively took all important decisions.

The decision arenas we have outlined are not self-contained and isolated from each other: they consist of the same political actors in different combinations. Hence they are *interrelated:* however, they are *fragmented* because they consist of different sets of these actors rather than a fully integrated and coordinated system, with clearly defined criteria for delegation from the full cabinet.

This model of interrelated but fragmented decision arenas might perhaps better be described as a framework rather than a model, since it has little explanatory power apart from the generalization that in modern cabinet systems the full cabinet is unable to take or even review all decisions made in the name of the government as a whole, and therefore requires a repertoire of formal and informal mechanisms for processing the majority of decisions not taken within departments. This framework does, however, allow for comparative analysis, in contrast to particularistic explanations of individual countries at particular points in time. One of the more depressing features of the British 'power of the Prime Minister' debate is its introversion, with little or no attempt to compare Britain with other countries with similar structures and use this as an opportunity to test whether propositions advanced in the British context appear to apply generally or whether special and perhaps unstated features of the British system are required to explain its operation.

As well as enabling comparison between countries of the role played by particular decision arenas such as cabinet committees and their relative importance within the overall structure of decision-making, this framework can be used to help analyse changes in decision-making arrangements across time within single countries and to investigate whether such variations are cyclical or constitute long-run trends. The importance of some of these decision arenas has grown in almost all countries in recent years, especially the role of cabinet committees. The cabinet committee system in Canada and the United Kingdom dates back to the Second World War. In other countries individual committees have had a lengthy existence: the Belgian Treasury Committee, the forerunner to the present day Committee for Economic and Social Coordination dates back to 1926 and the Netherlands Council for Economic Affairs was set up in 1945. But networks of committees in those countries and also in Denmark and Switzerland did not appear until the 1970s. Australia and New Zealand are in a midway position between these two groupings. The Australian committee system was set up under Chiffley's Labor government in 1945. The New Zealand system dates back to the 1950 National government headed by Sydney Holland.

However, this development is not simply a linear one, at least in terms of the number of committees. Christensen points to the reduction in the number of Danish committees in 1982 from twenty-five to fourteen (see chapter 7). A similar drastic reduction from fifteen to seven occurred in Belgium in the previous year. More generally, attempts to roll back committees have been made on several occasions. The Menzies government in Australia from 1950, the Diefenbaker government in Canada from 1957 to 1963, and the early years of the 1951 Churchill government in Britain were all marked by a determined attempt to downgrade the importance of committees.

Our framework can also be used as a starting point in investigating how far the use of different decision arenas varies according to whether there is a minority, a majority or a coalition government. In countries where coalition governments are common the informal multilateral arena seems to be preferred over formal cabinet committee structures. The Benelux countries, Germany, Switzerland and Italy arguably all fall into this group. *Experiments* in coalition government between novice allies whose previous relations were highly adversarial seem to have generated a more extensive use of formal committees: the Grand Coalition in Austria in 1945–66, the bourgeois coalition which followed decades of Labour government in Norway in 1965, the Liberal-Social Democrat administration in Denmark in 1978–9 are cases in point. The central role of the cabinet committee arena in four of the countries where single party majority government is the norm is also striking, though the fact that these countries are all Commonwealth nations prompts an alternative plausible explanation in terms of a diffusion theory of innovation.

The framework can also be used to compare decision-making as it affects different policy functions: for example, is education decision-making largely conducted within the unilateral decision arena to the same extent as appears to have been the case in Britain? Is public sector pay policy an issue that is always handled in cabinet committee or full cabinet?

In pointing to fragmentation of decision-making into a number of arenas, we would wish to contrast this with the emphasis that some writers on parliamentary systems have recently placed on the 'segmentation' or 'sectorization' of policy-making into a number of distinct and relatively self-contained policy areas or 'sectors', a literature providing a useful antidote to what might be called the 'full cabinet' model with its emphasis on a unified executive with a very high degree of integration and coordination (see, for example, Richardson and Jordan, 1979). Our point is rather different. Policy areas in any one country, and the overall pattern of decision-making in different countries, will vary in the extent to which policy areas (and particular issues) are distinct, and in the extent to which they are subject to decisions taken in unilateral, multilateral, cabinet committee, full cabinet, or other arenas. Some policy communities or sectors will largely involve discussion between interest groups and individual departments, while others, because of intrinsic characteristics or the allocation of functions between departments, will involve a number of departments in formal or informal discussions and will more frequently be the subject of consideration by a full cabinet.

The emphasis here on fragmentation might appear misplaced when compared with decision-making in the United States. Certainly compared with the United States, parliamentary systems with cabinet structures have a very high capacity for coordination, conflict resolution and authoritative decision-making *within the executive* (or at least within the executive and party structures in countries with coalitions). Much of this coordination and conflict resolution is carried out not by the full cabinet, however, but by arrangements lying between individual departments and the full cabinet, of which cabinet committees are clearly one of the most important, if hitherto much neglected, decision arenas.

References

Richardson, J.J. and A.G. Jordan (1979) *Governing Under Pressure*. Oxford: Martin Robertson.

Ridley, F. (1966) 'Chancellor Government as a Political System and the German Constitution', *Parliamentary Affairs*, 19: 446–61.

Seymour-Ure, C. (1971) 'The Disintegration of the Cabinet and the Neglected Issue of Cabinet Reform', *Parliamentary Affairs*, 24: 196–207.

Mayntz, R. (1980) 'Executive Leadership in Germany: Dispersion of Power or "*Kanzlerdemokratie*"?, in R. Rose and E. Suleiman (eds), *Presidents and Prime Ministers*. Washington DC: American Enterprise Institute.

II
CABINET STRUCTURES IN INDIVIDUAL COUNTRIES

4

The United Kingdom:
decision sifting in a secret garden

Brian W. Hogwood and Thomas T. Mackie

4.1 The evolution of cabinet government

The origins of the British cabinet can be traced back to Charles II's creation of a committee of members of the Privy Council to advise the king at the end of the seventeenth century. But the central characteristics of contemporary cabinet government in Britain owe much more to the constitutional and political changes of the nineteenth century. The principle that the cabinet should be responsible to Parliament and not the Crown developed slowly and was not generally accepted until the 1830s. After the 1932 Reform Act elections could no longer be successfully managed by the incumbent government and the cabinet became dependent on support in the House of Commons. The further expansion of the franchise in 1867 and 1884 was followed by the development of nationwide political parties. The cabinet became largely synonymous with the leading figures in the largest, usually majority, party in the House of Commons and political authority shifted from independent-minded members of parliament to party leadership. From the middle of the nineteenth century the cabinet has, with the exception of most of the two World Wars, almost always consisted of a single party. In peacetime the preferred option has usually been a minority government rather than a coalition when no party has enjoyed an overall majority (Butler, 1978: 112–13).

Since the middle of the nineteenth century the office of prime minister has been held by the leader of the party in government. The members of the government are chosen by the prime minister, and this is one of his or her most important prerogatives although the choices are restricted. The conventions that ministers should be members of parliament and nowadays be drawn overwhelmingly from the House of Commons and that senior appointments should usually go to those who have already served lengthy apprenticeships in more junior ministerial roles, dramatically limit the pool upon which he or she can draw (Rose, 1971). The prime minister does have more leeway in the allocation of portfolios and can substantially change the membership of the cabinet over the years.

The membership of the cabinet is only a subset of that of the government, which today may number more than a hundred persons. A few ministers are included in the cabinet who do not have formal departmental responsibilities. With the growth in the number of government departments in the twentieth century and especially after the Second World War, departmental ministers were often excluded from cabinet and attended cabinet meetings only when items of direct interest to their departments were on the agenda. The tendency to merge government departments into larger units with broader responsibilities which began in the 1950s has reversed this trend and all ministers who head departments are now routinely included in the cabinet.

The first cabinet committees were established in the middle of the nineteenth century. They were either ad hoc committees whose recommendations had to be endorsed by the full cabinet or legislative committees which were responsible for the drafting of individual government bills. It was not until the creation of the Committee of Imperial Defence in 1903 that the first *permanent* cabinet committee was set up. The First World War saw the creation of both a War Cabinet composed of a few key ministers and of a plethora of committees, but they were all abolished at the end of the war except for the Committee of Imperial Defence and the Home Affairs Committee, which dealt with the drafting of bills. The most important consequence of the First World War on the cabinet system was not the shortlived expansion of committees, but the establishment of a permanent cabinet secretariat, the Cabinet Office, which prepares the agenda and circulated papers for cabinet meetings.

The interwar period saw few changes from the pre-1914 pattern. A standing Finance Committee was set up in 1920 and in any one year there were in addition an average of twenty ad hoc committees (Gordon Walker, 1972: 39). During the Second World War a small War Cabinet of senior ministers was again created, supported by an extensive network of committees.

The 1945 Attlee government established a permanent system of cabinet committees which, like the cabinet itself, were serviced by the cabinet secretariat. Most authorities agree that the committee system established by Attlee set a pattern which has endured to the present day (Gordon Walker, 1972: 42; Rush, 1984: 45). However, only the Attlee government's network of committees has been comprehensively described (Hennessy and Arends, 1983). Unlike recent practice in other Commonwealth countries, the membership and even the existence of most cabinet committees is not made public. The creation or continuation of a committee, its chairmanship, composition and remit are the prerogative of the prime minister.

4.2 The number and functions of cabinet committees

The British government admits only to the existence of four standing committees of the cabinet (and even the announcements of these and the names of their chairmen was an innovation established by Mrs Thatcher in 1979). Following the 1983 General Election, it was announced in a Commons written answer that the cabinet committees and their chairmanship were as in Table 4.1. An important feature of the chairmanship of these standing committees, apart from the fact that Mrs Thatcher herself chairs two of them, is that none of them are chaired by departmental ministers.

However, this revealed information does not divulge the important role played by subcommittees of these standing committees, or ad hoc cabinet committees, to say nothing of the small, informal groups of ministers which appear to have played such an important role in decision-making under Mrs Thatcher. The existence of a committee on intelligence and security is also not mentioned.

Although the system has varied under each prime minister, since Attlee's government all British cabinets have had highly ramified systems of subcommittees and ad hoc committees. These ad hoc committees are alternately labelled MISC and GEN under succeeding government and are numbered in a continuous series which includes both ministerial and civil service committees. Hennessy (1984) estimated that Mrs Thatcher had established about twenty-five standing committees and about 110 ad hoc committees in her first five years of office, including committees of officials, of which he had details about forty-eight in addition to the four named standing committees. Mrs Thatcher's total is relatively modest compared to the 466 committees which the Attlee government accumulated in six and a quarter years and the 190 set up under the three years of the Callaghan government, though large compared to her apparent original intention to avoid having cabinet committees at all (Hennessy, 1984). However, in comparing the figures of different governments it is important to bear in mind the use of other devices, such as Mrs Thatcher's greater use of informal groups

TABLE 4.1
Officially announced standing committees of cabinet and their chairmen

Committee	Code letter	Chairman	Position of chairman
Home and Social Affairs	H	Lord Whitelaw	Lord President of the Council & Deputy Prime Minister
Economic Strategy	EA	Mrs Thatcher	Prime Minister
Oversea & Defence Policy	OD	Mrs Thatcher	Prime Minister
Legislation	L	John Biffen	Leader of the House of Commons

Source: *House of Commons Debates*, 4 July 1983, written answers.

of ministers, which might under other administrations have constituted formal cabinet committees.

At any given time, only a few of these committees will be meeting
regularly, and it is sometimes difficult to distinguish between the
functions of a subcommittee of a standing committee and an ad hoc
committee which deals with an issue which continues to attract the
attention of government. For example, the so called War Cabinet
on the Falklands War was a subcommittee (OD(SA)) of the
Oversea and Defence Committee though its work was temporary.
Similarly, H(HL) met only a few times to discuss the reform of the
House of Lords before deciding that nothing should be done
(Hennessy, 1984). On the other hand, the so called 'Star Chamber'
under Lord Whitelaw, which met each year from 1982 to try to
reconcile public expenditure bids which had not been resolved in
bilateral discussions between departments and the Treasury was an
ad hoc committee (MISC 62).

Secretarial support for the cabinet and cabinet committees is
provided through the Cabinet Office, with a secretariat of about 100
civil servants headed by the secretary of the cabinet. In 1982 the
secretary oversaw five secretariats, each headed by an under
secretary; they were responsible for overseas and defence matters,
economic affairs, home and parliamentary affairs, European affairs
and, finally, security and intelligence. Each secretariat services
several cabinet committees.

It is important to note that these committees comprise not only
committees of ministers, but also committees of civil servants.

TABLE 4.2
Partial list of ministerial cabinet committees in the Thatcher government
1979 to February 1985

Initials	Chairman	Post of chairman	Committee functions
		STANDING COMMITTEES	
Economic strategy committee and subcommittees			
EA	Thatcher	Prime Minister	Economic strategy, energy policy, changes in labour law, the most important EEC matters
E(EX)	Thatcher	Prime Minister	Exports policy
E(NI)	Thatcher	Prime Minister	Public sector strategy and oversight of the nationalized industries
E(NF)	Lawson	Chancellor of the Exchequer	Nationalized industry finance
E(PSP)	Lawson	Chancellor of the Exchequer	Public sector and public service pay policy
E(DL)	Lawson	Chancellor of the Exchequer	Disposal and privatization of state assets
E(PU)	Tebbit	Trade & Ind. Secretary	'Buy British' policy for public purchasing
E(CS)	Rees	Chief Secy. to the Treasury	Civil service pay and contingency plans for civil service strikes
Oversea and defence committee and subcommittees			
OD	Thatcher	Prime Minister	Foreign affairs, defence and Northern Ireland
OD(E)	Howe	Foreign Secretary	EEC policy
OD(SA)	Thatcher	Prime Minister	South Atlantic; the Falklands War Cabinet of 1982
OD(FOF)	Thatcher	Prime Minister	Future of the Falklands
Northern Ireland Group	Whitelaw	Lord President	Preparation of future initiatives
Home and social affairs committee and subcommittees			
H	Whitelaw	Lord President	Home affairs and social policy including education
H(HL)	Whitelaw	Lord President	Reform of House of Lords

Initials	Chairman	Post of chairman	Committee functions
Legislation committee			
L	Biffen	Leader of House of Commons	Future legislation and Queen's speech
Other standing committees			
CCU*	Brittan	Home Secretary	The Civil Contingencies Unit of the Cabinet Office; plans the maintenance of essential supplies and services during industrial disputes
HD	Brittan	Home Secretary	Civil defence
MIS	Thatcher	Prime Minister	Ministerial steering committee on intelligence which supervises MI5, MI6 and GCHQ and fixes budget priorities

AD HOC COMMITTEES

Initials	Chairman	Post of chairman	Committee functions
MISC 7	Thatcher	Prime Minister	Replacement of the Polaris force with Trident
MISC 14	Lawson	Chancellor of the Exchequer	Policy innovations
MISC 21	Whitelaw	Lord President	Meets each autumn to fix the level of rate and transport support grant for local authorities
MISC 62	Whitelaw	Lord President	The 'Star Chamber' for adjudicating on disputes about public expenditure allocations
MISC 79	Whitelaw	Lord President	Alternatives to domestic rates; rate-capping; also considered abolition of Greater London Council and metropolitan counties
MISC 87	Lawson	Chancellor of the Exchequer	De-indexing of benefits
MISC 91	Thatcher	Prime Minister	Choice of ALARM anti-radar missile
MISC 95	Thatcher	Prime Minister	Abolition of the Greater London Council and the metropolitan counties
MISC 101	Thatcher	Prime Minister	Response to developments in coal and dock strikes
?	?	?	Future of British Airways routes

Initials	Chairman	Post of chairman	Committee functions
?	King	Employment Secretary	Removal of obstacles, particularly to youth employment, including the exemption of workers under 18 from the Employment Protection Act, reducing employers' National Insurance contributions, modifying statutory sick pay, and increasing housing mobility
None	Thatcher	Prime Minister	Review of chemical weapons policy. Decided on 2 August 1984 not to restart production of nerve gases
?	Young	Minister without portfolio	Two committees examining deregulation and competition policy
MISC 107	? Young	Minister without portfolio	Employment and training of 14–18 year olds
MISC 108	Young	Minister without portfolio	Small firms
?	Thatcher	Prime Minister	Review of how 'Star Chamber' (MISC 62) might be involved at earlier stage of annual public expenditure decision cycle
?	Thatcher	Prime Minister	Examining report based on work of four committees reviewing social security. Met weekly from 6 February 1985
?	?	?	Studying plans for legislation to allow Crown Estate Commissioners to renovate and let out part of Hampton Court Palace
?	Young	Minister without portfolio	Development of tourism and leisure

Note: * 'Mixed committee' containing both ministers and civil servants.
Sources: Hennessy (1984), *Times*, *Financial Times*, *Sunday Times*, *New Statesman*, *Economist*.

These committees are a part of the cabinet *system* insofar as they are serviced by the Cabinet Office, but it is important to note that there are also interdepartmental committees which are not part of the formal cabinet office network but which nevertheless play an important role in decision-making; for example, the interdepartmental committee of civil servants which conducted a major review of regional policy prior to the White Paper on regional policy in 1983 was chaired by a Treasury official.

The role of interdepartmental committees is disputed. Such committees are often described as simply working for ministers and making recommendations or identifying options for cabinet committees (Morrison, 1954: 26; Wilson, 1976: 101). However, other ministers have argued that their role is more considerable. Crossman (1975: 200) argues, for instance, that:

> very often the whole job is pre-cooked in the official committees to a point from which it is extremely difficult to reach any other conclusion than that already determined by the officials in advance... I have yet to see a Minister prevail against an inter-departmental official paper without the backing of a Prime Minister, a First Secretary or the Chancellor.

The same point has also been made by Benn (1980: 86; see also Hennessy, 1982b).

The cabinet secretary, in addition to acting as secretary to the full cabinet and to cabinet committees chaired by the prime minister, frequently exercises a more personal influence on the prime minister as a result of the frequently close personal links which have developed between the prime minister and his civil servants (Seldon, 1981: 108, 118; Crossman, 1976: 296; Campbell, 1983; Hennessy, 1980).

Despite the importance placed in British constitutional doctrine on ministerial responsibility and accountability, all British governments have made use of mixed committees of ministers and civil servants. The Conservative government of 1970–4 was led by Edward Heath, who felt that the cabinet committee system had got out of hand and made extensive use of mixed committees of ministers and civil servants (Hennessy, 1983a; Fay and Young, 1976: 8–9). A problem with such committees was the unwillingness of civil servants to disagree with their ministers. The use of such mixed committees was cut back under the subsequent Labour government of Harold Wilson. The Callaghan government of 1976–9, after extensive discussion of economic strategy in full cabinet at the time of the IMF loan in 1976, made use of a mixed group of ministers (Dennis Healey, Chancellor of the Exchequer, Harold Lever, Chancellor of the Duchy of Lancaster) and officials (the prime minister's principal private secretary and the heads of the Treasury, Bank of England, the Cabinet Office and the Central Policy Review Staff) (Hennessy, 1983a).

TABLE 4.3
Membership of three cabinet committees

Initials and function	Chairman	Other members	Post
OD(SA)* Falklands War Cabinet	Thatcher, Prime Minister	Whitelaw	Home Secretary and Deputy Prime Minister
		Pym	Foreign Secretary
		Nott	Defence Secretary
		Parkinson	Paymaster General (and Chairman of Conservative Party)
MISC 62 Public Expenditure 'Star Chamber'	Whitelaw Lord President and Deputy Prime Minister	Younger	Scottish Secretary
		Rees	Chief Secretary
		Biffen	Leader of Commons**
		Brittan	Home Secretary**
Review of chemical weapons policy	Thatcher, Prime Minister	Heseltine	Defence Secretary
		Howe	Foreign Secretary
		Lawson	Chancellor of the Exchequer
		Brittan	Home Secretary
		Whitelaw	Lord President and Deputy PM
		Biffen	Leader of Commons

Notes: * There was also an official team consisting of Sir Terence Lewin (Chief of the Defence Staff), Sir Anthony Acland (Permanent Secretary at the Foreign Office), Sir Robert Armstrong (Cabinet Secretary), and Robert Wade-Gery (head of foreign and defence liaison in the Cabinet Office. Sir Michael Palliser, outgoing Permanent Secretary at the Foreign Office headed a 'communications group' within the Cabinet Office.
** And a former Chief Secretary to the Treasury.
Sources: Seymour-Ure (1984); Hastings and Jenkins (1983); *Times*, 15 October 1984; *New Statesman*, 11 January 1985; *Times*, 11 January 1985.

4.3 **The composition of committees**

Given that the very existence of all other than four standing cabinet committees is kept secret, it is not surprising that there is no systematic information about the membership or criteria for determining composition. Table 4.3 lists the members of three cabinet committees under the Thatcher government for which the full membership is known. The Falklands War Cabinet contained both the main ministers with direct functional responsibilities, plus the party leadership (prime minister, deputy prime minister and chairman of the Conservative Party).

The Star Chamber is very unusual in that it is deliberately designed to exclude those ministers whose departments are most affected by its decisions. The Secretary of State for Scotland, though a spending minister, does not have a vested interest in any given bid, since the bulk of the change to his department's expenditure is linked to change in the corresponding English departments, and can then be reallocated within his own total (Heald, 1983: 247). The remaining members of the committee, apart from the chairman who is not a departmental minister, were the Chief Secretary to the Treasury (the minister directly concerned with controlling public expenditure), and two of his predecessors. Thus the membership was determined on functional grounds, but this example emphasizes that 'functional' should not be equated with having representatives from the departments most directly affected.

The committee which reviewed chemical weapons policy in 1984 seems, like the Falklands War Cabinet, to contain a mixture of ministers from departments most involved and cabinet members who could act as a sounding board for likely party opinion outside cabinet (Whitelaw for the Lords and Biffen for the Commons).

The evidence from this limited and perhaps untypical sample is that functional considerations (though not necessarily functional representation) dominate in selecting committee membership, and there is no evidence of concern to ensure that committees are balanced in terms of ideology or any other basis of representation such as territory.

A former British permanent secretary has argued that the allocation of departmental responsibilities and cabinet committee membership enabled the 'monetarists' to dominate the 1979 Thatcher government on economic matters:

> The monetarist minority nevertheless prevailed in economic and industrial policy because they had strategic control of the key Departments and *Cabinet committees*; as in previous administrations, only the Prime Minister and Treasury Ministers were effectively involved in taxation policy and, in conjunction with the Bank of England, in interest

rates and exchange policy. *The doubters and dissenters were either given no opportunity to mount a challenge in full Cabinet or were unable to do so effectively* (Pliatzky, 1981: 178; emphasis added).

The key decision to proceed with a British atomic bomb was taken in cabinet committee reconstituted to exclude ministerial opponents of the bomb. At a meeting of the relevant cabinet committee (GEN 75) on 25 October 1946 Dalton, the Chancellor of the Exchequer, and Cripps, the President of the Board of Trade, voiced opposition to developing the bomb, doubting whether the economy could afford it or whether it v,as needed. They were defeated on that occasion, but only by the late arrival of Bevin, the Foreign Secretary. When the time approached to take a final decision, Dalton and Cripps were excluded from the relevant committee by the device of replacing GEN 75 by a new committee, GEN 163, which met without them on 10 January 1947 (Hennessy, 1982a). This again illustrates the ability of the British prime minister to skew membership of cabinet committees.

The appointment of the committee chairman is particularly important in the British system given the lack of formal votes and the key role of the chairman in summing up the decision of the committee (see especially Gordon Walker, 1972: 119–20; Kaufman, 1981: 72). For example, in 1978 the cabinet committee on energy (ENM) was chaired not by the left-wing energy minister, Tony Benn, but by the more right-wing industry minister, Eric Varley (Page, 1978: 74).

One way of attempting to ascertain whether personal or functional considerations predominate is to examine whether the chairmanship of cabinet committees changes when the holder of the office of the original chairman changes. Table 4.4 presents information on this for committees where the chairmanship in both 1982 and 1984 is known. Interpretation of this information is made difficult by the fact that William Whitelaw (now Lord Whitelaw) wore two 'hats' before 1983, one as Home Secretary and one as Deputy Prime Minister. The table would, however, appear to indicate that there are two different types of committee in terms of the determination of the chairmanship. The first type, which includes a number of economic subcommittees chaired by the Chancellor of the Exchequer, the subcommittee on civil service matters, the subcommittee on EEC matters, the Central Contingencies Unit and the standing committee on future legislation, have 'functional' chairmen, that is chairmen holding a ministerial office which has the main or an important responsibility for the subjects discussed by the committee. When the minister leaves that office he or she is replaced as chairman of the relevant committees by his or her successor as minister. The second type of committee consists of those chaired by a minister who does not head a department, or who is acting in a non-departmental capacity, such as deputy prime minister; such a minister may continue as chairman even if part of his or her ministerial responsibilities is changed — this was the case with most of the committees chaired by Whitelaw in both 1982 and 1984, even though he had ceased to be Home Secretary.

The constitutional distinction between the role of ministers and that of civil servants is *generally* reflected in the cabinet committee system. Of the top civil servants interviewed by Campbell (1983: 279), only 15 per cent regularly attended ministerial committees, whereas nearly 90 per cent were routinely in non-ministerial committees. Moreover, their role in ministerial committees was mostly that of observer or adviser, rarely that of a full discussant. This suggests that the form that this participation may take is to give expert advice in committees dealing with technical questions which were exceptionally complex. For instance, Richard Crossman (1976: 286) records that Treasury and Social Security civil servants were involved in the cabinet committee on pensions which he chaired. However, civil servants are full members of the emergency committee of the cabinet (COBRA), which dealt, for instance, with highly politically sensitive questions such as the siege of the Iranian Embassy, and senior Whitehall figures were routinely involved in the Falklands War Cabinet (Seymour-Ure, 1984: 187).

4.4 Decision arenas in the United Kingdom executive

4.4.1 *Unilateral*
Most government decisions are made within the confines of single government departments. Most of these are, of course, detailed decisions about the implementation of agreed government policy. Such decisions can, however, be quite important individually.

The extent to which important decisions, including policy decisions, can be made within individual departments will vary according to a number of factors, including the way in which portfolios were initially divided up and intrinsic characteristics of the functions of the department which will determine the extent to which they interact with the functions of other departments. A number of former euducation ministers have commented on how most of the decisions relating to education (other than negotiations with the Treasury about finance) were taken within the education department (see Kogan, 1971; Butler and Crowther-Hunt, 1965). For example, Anthony Crosland, who served both as trade minister and education minister in the Labour government of 1964–70, pointed out that in the trade ministry almost every issue that came up involved other departments — the Treasury, the Department of

TABLE 4.4
Change in office holding and chairmanship of cabinet committees

Initials	1982		1984	
	Chairman	Office	Chairman	Office
E(NF)	Howe	Chancellor	Lawson	Chancellor
E(PSP)	Howe	Chancellor	Lawson	Chancellor
E(DL)	Howe	Chancellor	Lawson	Chancellor
E(CS)	Young	Civil Service	Rees	Chief Secy. to Treasury*
OD(E)	Carrington	Foreign	Howe	Foreign
N. Ireland	Whitelaw	Home and Deputy PM	Whitelaw	Ld. Presid. and Deputy PM
QL or L	Pym	Leader of Commons	Biffen	Leader of Commons
H	Whitelaw	Home and Deputy PM	Whitelaw	Ld. Presid. and Deputy PM
CCU	Whitelaw	Home and Deputy PM	Brittan	Home
MISC 14	Howe	Chancellor	Lawson	Chancellor
MISC 21	Whitelaw	Home and Deputy PM	Whitelaw	Ld. Presid. and Deputy PM
MISC 62	Whitelaw	Home and Deputy PM	Whitelaw	Ld. Presid. and Deputy PM

Note: * The Civil Service Department was abolished in November 1982 and its functions split between the Treasury and the new Manpower and Personnel Office.
Source: Based on information in Hennessy (1982, 1984).

Economic Affairs, Housing and Local Government, Scotland and Wales, but that education was a particularly independent department. Another minister in the 1964–70 Labour government, Roy Jenkins (1971), who served as Home Secretary and Chancellor of the Exchequer, commented on how few of the decisions involving the Home Secretary involved collective ministerial discussion, but that the work of the Treasury was intrinsically interdepartmental.

Crosland also drew attention to another factor which leads to a large number of issues being taken within departments:

> The other thing is that if you're carrying out agreed Party policy, and seem to be doing it reasonably successfully and without frightful rows breaking out, your colleagues won't particularly want to interfere. They are all exceedingly busy men in their own jobs, and I think they were prepared to trust my judgement (Kogan, 1971: 160–1).

Decision-making is often less than strictly unilateral: it is often the product of negotiation between a department and relevant groups. Even if the cabinet or cabinet committees subsequently formally consider proposals from the department concerned, there may be little scope for unwinding any deal struck between the department and the group (see e.g. Butler and Crowther-Hunt, 1965).

4.4.2 *Internalized coordination*

Occasionally, prime ministers have attempted to introduce individual ministers as coordinators over departments headed by other ministers. One such attempt was the introduction by Churchill of a number of 'overlords' responsible for coordinating a number of related departments. This experiment is generally considered to have failed since it blurred ministerial responsibility for departments, and it was abandoned in 1953 (Gordon Walker, 1972; Jones, 1975). These 'overlords' were appointed on top of the existing departmental ministers rather than being heads of departments themselves. An interesting exception is the Minister of Defence after the Second World War, who did have his own department while the War Office, Admiralty, and Air Ministry continued. The three service departments were merged into the Ministry of Defence in the early 1960s.

Other ministers with 'coordinating' functions may be appointed. For example, Britain normally has a minister responsible for coordinating government information services. Ministers without departmental responsibilities may be given broader responsibility for assisting the coordination of a number of sets of related functions, as was Shirley Williams as Paymaster General in Britain in the 1974–9 Labour government. However, this role is exercised not at an individual or simply interdepartmental level, but by giving such ministers the chairmanship of cabinet committees, and is thus part of the process of resolving issues in such committees (Jones, 1975: 42).

4.4.3 *Bilateral*

Many of the key decisions affecting a department, namely those concerning programme finance, are the subject of bilateral negotiation between the spending department and the Treasury. The full cabinet determines the ceiling within which allocations are to be made and perhaps set broad guidelines, and it (or a special cabinet committee) may act as a court of appeal where the spending department and the Treasury are unable to reach agreement, but the cabinet will not normally review allocations which have been agreed in bilateral negotiations between spending departments and the Treasury.

Another important set of bilateral links within the cabinet framework is between the prime minister and a few key ministers, particularly the Chancellor of the Exchequer and the Foreign Secretary. Prime ministers tend to devote a much larger proportion of their time to foreign affairs than to the work of other departments and many issues may be discussed between the prime minister and the Foreign Secretary without ever being brought to the attention of other ministers (see, e.g., Rose, 1980: 335–8; Gordon Walker, 1972: 88, 116).

On the annual Budget (which in Britain deals only with taxation), the Chancellor of the Exchequer closely consults the prime minister, but other ministers normally have to accept a fait accompli. Individual ministers may be consulted by the Chancellor about tax changes relating to their departmental concerns. Under the Thatcher Conservative government other ministers reacted strongly to their total exclusion in 1981 from tax decision-making, but while they were subsequently given an opportunity to state their view in general terms about economic strategy the process of tax decision-making does not appear to have been altered.

4.4.4 *Multilateral*

We have already noted in 4.2 that there is a complex network of interdepartmental committees outside the cabinet committee struc- ture, mainly interdepartmental committees of officials rather than ministers, but this is only the most formal aspect of multilateral contacts. Noting that the multiplicity of policy decisions requiring interdepartmental clearance is far greater than could be handled in cabinet or even cabinet committee meetings in Britain, Pliatzky (1981: 36–7) states that:

> A great deal of business is therefore carried out by inter-Ministerial correspondence: it is in fact rather exceptional for one individual Minister to write to another individual Minister and almost always his letter is copied to, say, half a dozen other Ministers, or to the rather large number of Ministers who make up a Cabinet committee, or to all the members of Cabinet. The photocopier is nowadays both literally and figuratively an essential element in the machinery of government. Even so the system could not work without the technocratic back-up, whether working through official committees run by the Cabinet Office or other inter-Departmental committees, or the network of informal contacts between officials.

A number of departments may be involved in the implementation of some policies because of functional interaction, or because special arrangements are made for administration of the policy in

Scotland, Wales and Northern Ireland. In such cases there will be a number of sets of committees with varying combinations of representatives from the departments or agencies sponsored by them. In addition, one department may be designated the 'lead' department. This department is given the responsibility for drawing together any proposals for changes in policy, but only after consultation with other departments involved. For example, the Department of Trade and Industry is the lead department for regional policy, even though it only administers the policy in England (Hogwood, 1982).

4.4.5 *Cabinet committees*
The authority of British cabinet committees and their role as the effective taker of final decisions was increased by the ruling in 1967 by the then Prime Minister, Harold Wilson, that a matter could be taken to the cabinet from a committee only with the agreement of the committee chairman (who is appointed by the prime minister). In theory, ministers still had the constitutional right to bring any matter to the cabinet, including a question settled in a committee, but 'in practice this right was greatly attenuated' (Gordon Walker, 1972: 44; see also Kaufman, 1981: 69). In exercising his or her discretion, the chairman was expected to consider the degree of disagreement in the committee or the intrinsic importance of the issue or its political overtones. A dispute between an aggrieved minister and the chairman of the committee over referring an issue to full cabinet would be resolved by the prime minister. Based on his own experience, Patrick Gordon Walker (1972: 119) emphasized that 'it is the chairman's duty to try and settle things in committee and as far as possible save the time of the Cabinet.' Even where there is disagreement, the committee chairman may refer the matter back for reconsideration by individual ministers and only refer it to cabinet if disagreement persists.

Although each new government can define its own rules for cabinet committee procedure, and the 'Wilson ruling' was not continued by the incoming Conservative government in 1970, the ruling appears to encapsulate the reality of practice under most recent British governments. For example, under the 1974–9 Labour government the prime minister would rarely allow ministers to bring matters settled in committee to full cabinet; even in the case of an exceptionally influential minister this had to be on a matter of major importance. Under the Heath government of 1970–4, however, it appears that 'all Cabinet committee decisions, even non-controversial ones, were reported to the Cabinet, giving ministers who had not been closely involved the opportunity to have their say

(*Times*, 7 February 1984), though it is not clear how often ministers availed themselves of this opportunity.

The status of cabinet committee decisions which are not discussed in full cabinet in Britain seems quite clear:

> Cabinet committees are parallel and equal to the Cabinet itself. In matters within their terms of reference, committees can come to a decision that has the same authority as a Conclusion of the Cabinet: it will be accepted and acted upon as if it were a Cabinet decision (Gordon Walker, 1972: 119).

Other former British cabinet ministers have also confirmed that 'a lot is settled at Cabinet Committees without having to go to the Cabinet' and that 'A lot of the big defence issues will be decided by the Chiefs of Staff, and by the Defence Committee, and they would not themselves come to the Cabinet except for confirmation' (Butler and Crowther-Hunt, 1965: 194; see also Kaufman, 1981: 69, 72).

One of the potential dangers with a system of permitting cabinet committees to make final decisions is that a minority in the committee might be overruled yet be potentially capable of mobilizing a majority in the full cabinet. It is an especial danger that in any conflict involving a dispute about public expenditure between a spending minister and the budget minister that the budget minister will be outvoted in committee by a coalition of spending ministers, whereas in full cabinet he or she may be able to rely on the support of the prime minister and other non-spending ministers. In Britain an important change in the mechanisms for resolving this problem took place in 1976 (see Pliatzky, 1982: 140–1; Barnet, 1982: 18). Prior to that date treasury ministers had a long-standing right to reserve their position in cabinet committees on financial matters and take them to full cabinet. Treasury ministers had to be selective in choosing which issues to take to full cabinet, since, as a former Treasury minister put it, 'taking issues to Cabinet all the time would not endear me to the Prime Minister' (Barnett, 1982: 27). However, from 1976 the rule was that Treasury ministers could not be overruled in cabinet committees on financial matters. In other words, the Treasury no longer had to reserve its position, and the onus was shifted to the relevant spending minister to take his case to cabinet. (Information about this important change relates specifically to the Labour government which left office in 1979.)

It should not be assumed that cabinet committees will deal with low-level issues and that all important decisions will be dealt with in full cabinet. There can be few more important decisions than whether and how to launch or curtail major military operations, yet in Britain these are more likely to be handled by a cabinet committee than by full cabinet (see Seymour-Ure, 1984). The handling of the war between Britain and Argentina over the Falkland Islands in 1982 was supervised by a committee variously referred to as the Inner Cabinet, the War Cabinet and the Falklands groups of ministers. A similar cabinet committee performed a similar role in the Suez Crisis of 1956, with the prime minister and the Foreign Secretary making arrangements on some key matters (Gordon Walker, 1972: 90; Mackintosh, 1977: 24–5; Seymour-Ure, 1984).

One of the most momentus sets of decisions taken by British cabinet committees rather than full cabinet was that concerned with the development of the British nuclear deterrent (see also 4.3). Particularly notable about this set of decisions was the way in which cabinet was not merely almost completely excluded from all the major discussions on atomic policy in 1945–51 but was not even kept informed of decisions taken in cabinet committees (Gowing, 1974: 20). However, under the subsequent Churchill government the full cabinet did have the opportunity to discuss the proposal to develop a hydrogen bomb (*Times*, 3 January 1985).

Cabinet committees, then, perform the decisive role in the process of arriving at many government decisions. They can, to use Gordon Walker's (1972: 87–91) term, be seen as 'partial cabinets'.

4.4.6 *Cabinet*

We argued in chapter 1 that in practice cabinets rarely take on the role of setting strategic guidelines for government policy in explicit form. There have, however, been occasions when full cabinet in Britain has participated in extensive discussion of strategic policy-making. In its first few years the Heath government of 1970–4 held six-monthly meetings with members of the Central Policy Review Staff, the government's think tank based in the Cabinet Office, to review the extent to which the government was keeping to its originally stated strategy. However, this did not prevent the government's economic policies from undergoing dramatic changes.

An exceptional case was the extensive discussion under the Callaghan government in 1976 of the government's application for an IMF loan (see Hennessy, 1983a; Granada Television, 1977: 49–61). A total of twenty-six meetings of the full cabinet discussed the implications. However, the cabinet had to rely extensively on reports of the prime minister and the Chancellor of the Exchequer on their discussions with the IMF and foreign governments — *the full cabinet did not and could not have conducted the negotiations with the IMF en masse.* The views of the prime minister and the Chancellor about what would be acceptable to the IMF and foreign governments, and the prime minister's personal interest in securing a sterling 'safety net' were crucial in winning the support of otherwise reluctant cabinet ministers. Further, once the cabinet had approved the principle of the loan and the accompanying economic policy approach, the details were worked out outside the full cabinet. Subsequent strategic economic policy discussions under the Callaghan government were undertaken by a mixed group of ministers and officials (see 4.2 above).

In chapter 1 we outlined one of the roles of full cabinets as being the selective review of decisions of cabinet committees. Jones (1975: 49) argues that:

> a Cabinet committee realizes that its decisions will be acceptable only if it has the support of the Cabinet which can reject or refer back or amend them. The authority of a Cabinet committee comes from the fact that its members might be able to influence the Cabinet on a particular item.

This assertion seems to us to overlook the significance of the fact that matters resolved in cabinet committees cannot always be reopened in full cabinet, though the practice has varied under recent British governments. Matters may not even be placed on the cabinet agenda. The full cabinet may simply not have the opportunity to 'reject or refer back or amend' such decisions.

Nevertheless, commentators, ministers and civil servants may believe in the importance of 'anticipated reactions' and this belief may itself give the idea some practical force. Hennessy (1983b) reports one cabinet minister who was not on the cabinet committee managing the Falklands War in 1982 as claiming that the prime minister had to carry all cabinet ministers on all major decisions and that the naval task force would never have sailed without cabinet approval, and another 'Whitehall figure' claiming that the reason why there was no cabinet committee on trade union reform consisting solely of Mrs Thatcher and her sympathizers on this issue was that what they produced would not have got past the cabinet.

Both the contents and the position of an item on the cabinet agenda are strongly influenced by the prime minister. For example, if an item comes up a few minutes before the end of a cabinet meeting a matter can be dealt with very speedily in the way the prime minister wants.

In Britain the major decision-making role of cabinet is as resolver of controversial issues that cabinet committees have been unable to resolve, or which go straight to cabinet. Jones (1975: 31) argues that 'for the most politically important issues the cabinet is the effective decision-making body' and the fact that non-controversial points are cleared away strengthens the role of cabinet because it can then concentrate on the undetermined items. However, the significance of this in policy-making terms depends on the definitions of 'political importance' and 'non-controversial'. Jones makes it clear that:

> politically important issues ... may not be the most 'objectively' or 'intrinsically' important, particularly in terms of their long-run implications, but they are the most contentious at the time.

Other commentators and former cabinet ministers have similarly distinguished between 'politically significant' and 'objectively significant' decisions, with the cabinet taking decisions on the former but not necessarily on the latter (see e.g. Seymour-Ure, 1971: 202; Crosland in Kogan, 1971: 161).

It is by no means apparent that the British cabinet system in any case is very effective at ensuring that politically sensitive issues are filtered up to the full cabinet. A number of examples from 1983–4 confirm this. For two years running, the annual public expenditure review as announced in the autumn included decisions not considered by the full cabinet (housing benefits in 1983 and student grants in 1984) which proved to be so politically sensitive that the government (unusually for a British government with a large overall majority in the House of Commons) had to announce partial reversal of the policy soon thereafter. That the failure to discuss politically sensitive issues was not confined to the overload associated with reviewing all public expenditure was confirmed by the decision taken in early 1984 to ban trade unions from the government's intelligence communications headquarters in Cheltenham. This decision was taken initially by Mrs Thatcher, the Prime Minister, Sir Geoffrey Howe, the Foreign Secretary and Michael Hesletine, the Secretary of State for Defence (*Times*, 7 February 1984). Lord Whitelaw, in charge of presentation of government policies, and Tom King, the Secretary of State for Employment were involved later. The lack of discussion in Cabinet was confirmed by Sir Geoffrey Howe:

> It was discussed, as almost every government decision is discussed, by the group of ministers most directly involved ... There are very few discussions of government decisions by full Cabinet (*Times*, 7 February 1984, citing *Daily Mail*, 6 February 1984).

Even the prime minister may not be aware of what subsequently transpire to be politically sensitive issues, as the former Labour Prime Minister, James Callaghan, discovered to his embarrassment in April 1984 when he challenged a Conservative government decision that the Metropolitan Police should be allowed to buy sub-machine guns. It transpired that the original decision had been taken under his own administration in August 1976, and that the decision had been taken by the Home Secretary of the time without being considered in cabinet or cabinet committee or being referred to the prime minister.

Given that the cabinet committee system is designed to avoid overloading the full cabinet, some issues which it is difficult to classify as scoring high on either 'objective' or 'politically sensitive' factors do nevertheless appear to take up the time of full cabinet. The Churchill cabinet in 1954 discussed what they considered to be the alarming growth of 'unnatural offences of the gravest kind', namely sodomy and bestiality, 'the amount of soliciting by prostitutes in some parts of central London', and whether Princess Margaret should cease to have a destroyer escort when she flew across an expanse of sea (*Times*, 4 January 1985). The Prime Minister found time to intervene to try to prevent a takeover bid for the Savoy Hotel and had to be restrained from travelling to Gibraltar to provide 'ministerial cover' to welcome the arrival of the Queen in Gibraltar at the end of a Commonwealth tour.

While we accept the point that the full cabinet does not normally consider non-politically sensitive issues, we do not agree that as a result politically sensitive issues are inevitably channeled up to full cabinet for discussion. Indeed, some issues, such as the decision to ban trade unions from the communications headquarters at Cheltenham, may be considered *too sensitive* for discussion in full cabinet. There may even be explicit attempts to push responsibility for sensitive issues back to other decision arenas, as in the November 1984 public expenditure review at a time when the Ethiopian famine was attracting public attention, when the Treasury claimed that decisions on the total size of the overseas aid budget were a matter for the Foreign Secretary within the total amount allocated to him.

Even when issues do go to full cabinet it tends to be individual issues and not consideration of policy areas. For example, cabinet may be asked to take a decision about the closure of an individual industrial plant rather than to reappraise all aspects of regional policy. In dealing with politically important issues, cabinet members inevitably have a fragmentary picture of the broader policy context in which the issues have arisen.

4.4.7 *Party*

Britain has not had a coalition government since the Second World War, but there has been one period of inter-party collaboration which is interesting for what did *not* happen in terms of executive decison-making as much as what did. Between March 1977 and May 1978 there was an agreement, popularly known as the Lib-Lab Pact, between the Labour government, which had lost its overall parliamentary majority in 1976, and the Liberal Party (Mitchie and Hoggart, 1978; Steel, 1980). The agreement provided for informal consultations between individual ministers and Liberal spokesmen, and a Joint Consultative Committee with an open membership, chaired by Michael Foot, then leader of the House of Commons and Lord President of the Council, to resolve any unsolved differences. The Committee was meant to meet fortnightly, but in fact met less frequently, with meetings averaging one a month during the first nine months of the pact. As had been intended, the bulk of consultation on individual topics took place between ministers and individual Liberal spokesmen. It is important to stress that these meetings were additional to and not a substitute for the normal consideration of issues within the executive in departments, in cabinet committees and in cabinet, from all of which the Liberals were excluded. In this context it is worth noting that the Joint Consultative Committee was serviced by the Lord President's Office and, in contrast to cabinet committees proper, *not* by the Cabinet Office.

Intra-party politics is an informal decision-making arena, the importance of which may vary both according to the partisan composition of the government and between governments of the same party. Although rarely resulting in actual defeats for governments with overall majorities, there has been an upsurge in the assertiveness of backbenchers since the early 1970s (Norton, 1980). Reflecting both this and perhaps the poor relations between government supporters and her predecessor in 1970–4, Edward Heath, Mrs Thatcher has maintained close contact with the executive of the backbench Conservative 1922 Committee and ministers have been encouraged to put policy proposals before the relevant backbench policy committees (Burch, 1983, 409). These arrangements did not prevent a series of breakdowns in communications and ministerial *faux pas* at the end of 1984 and the beginning of 1985. It should be stressed that Conservative backbenchers have not been involved in actual decision-making. The concern has been to sound out opinion in advance so that party reaction, among a number of other considerations, can be taken into account in the arenas in which decisions are actually taken. The evidence suggests that ministers are not always accurate in assessing in advance which are likely to be the issues on which backbench and wider party opinion is likely to be sensitive. There is certainly nothing amounting to a central party clearing-house.

To provide links with the extra-parliamentary party, the Chairman of the Conservative Party (appointed by the party leader) has often been made a member of the cabinet (and may also hold substantive ministerial office). This informal connection is impossible in the Labour Party since the party standing orders forbid the General Secretary (who is appointed by the National Executive Committee (NEC) rather than the Parliamentary party or the party leader) from sitting in the House of Commons and thus effectively from cabinet membership. During the 1974–6 Wilson government a Liaison Committee consisting of ministers nominated by the prime minister and Executive members elected by the party's NEC met regularly. The prime minister and leading ministers, plus the chief whip, met the General Secretary and the chairperson and the vice-chairperson of the NEC nearly every week (Wilson, 1976, 164). In addition, ministers were asked to attend meetings of NEC sub-committees whose remit was relevant to their responsibilities (Kaufman, 1980, 112).

Overall, then, the British experience is not one of party integration into executive decision-making but of party influence through the executive making arrangements for liaison or through anticipated reactions. A major role of party is through the development of policies in Opposition which then contribute to the agendas of the various decision arenas in the first few years after the party achieves office.

4.5 Conclusion

Since the Second World War the British government has always had a highly ramified system of standing cabinet committees, subcommittees and ad hoc committees, though the bulk of government decisions are made in individual departments or through interdepartmental negotiations outside the cabinet structure. The use which is made of the full cabinet, cabinet committees and more informal groupings of ministers and political advisers has varied between governments, reflecting largely the decision-making style of individual prime ministers. These individual differences appear to have been more important than differences between the two parties which have held office since 1945.

The full cabinet does not necessarily consider all issues which are important on 'objective' indicators such as financial cost or number of persons affected. Supposedly, this leaves the cabinet free to consider the most politically sensitive issues. However, we have suggested that the British cabinet system is poor at filtering out issues which are potentially very politically sensitive but which are not structured in terms of conflict between two or more departments. Where the sponsoring department is satisfied in its own mind (or has done a deal with the Treasury if it is an issue involving expenditure), then the cabinet may only consider the issue *after* the political alarm bells have started ringing and may not be involved in taking the actual decision to resolve the problem.

References

Barnett, J. (1982) *Inside the Treasury*. London: Andre Deutsch.

Benn, T. (1980) 'Manifestos and Mandarins', pp. 57–78 in Royal Institute of Public Administration, *Policy and Practice: The Experience of Government*. London: Royal Institute of Public Administration.

Burch, M. (1983) 'Mrs Thatcher's Approach to Leadership in Government: 1979–June 1983', *Parliamentary Affairs*, 36: 399–416.

Butler, D. (1978) *Coalitions in British Politics*. London: Macmillan.

Butler, Lord and Lord Crowther-Hunt (1965) 'Reflections on Cabinet Government', *The Listener*, 16 September 1965, 407–11 (reprinted in V. Herman and J. Alt (eds), *Cabinet Studies: A Reader*. London: Macmillan, 1975, 193–209).

Campbell, C. (1983) *Governments under Stress: Political Executives and Key Bureaucrats in Washington, London and Ottawa*. Toronto: University of Toronto Press.

Crossman, R. (1975) *The Diaries of a Cabinet Minister: Volume One: Minister of Housing 1964–66*. London: Hamish Hamilton and Jonathan Cape.

Crossman, R. (1976) *The Diaries of a Cabinet Minister: Volume Two: Lord President of the Council and Leader of the House of Commons 1966–68*. London: Hamish Hamilton and Jonathan Cape.

Fay, S. and H. Young (1976) *The Fall of Heath*. London: The Sunday Times.

Gowing, M. (1974) *Independence and Deterrence: Britain and Atomic Energy, 1945–52: Volume I: Policy Making*. London: Macmillan.

Granada Television (1977) *Inside British Politics*. London and Manchester: Granada Television.

Hastings, M. and S. Jenkins (1983) *The Battle for the Falklands*. London: Michael Joseph.

Heald, D. (1983) *Public Expenditure*. Oxford: Martin Robertson.

Hennessy, P. (1980) 'Committee Decided Callaghan Economic Policy', *The Times*, 17 March 1980.

Hennessy, P. (1982a) 'How Bevin Saved Britain's Bomb', *The Times*, 30 September 1982.

Hennessy, P. (1982b) 'Document Access Inquiry Troubles Whitehall', *The Times*, 13 November 1982.

Hennessy, P. (1983a) 'Is Tradition of Cabinet Government on the Wane?' *The Times*, 16 May 1983.

Hennessy, P. (1983b) 'Shades of a Home Counties Boudicca', *The Times*, 17 May 1983.

Hennessy, P. (1984) 'Whitehall's Real Power House', *The Times*, 30 April 1984.

Hennessy, P. and A. Arends (1983) *Mr Attlee's Engine Room*. Strathclyde Papers on Government and Politics, No. 26. Glasgow: Department of Politics, University of Strathclyde.

Hogwood, B. W. (1982) 'In Search of Accountability: the Territorial Dimension of Industrial Policy', *Public Administration Bulletin*, 38: 22–39.

Jenkins, R. (1981) 'On Being a Minister', *Sunday Times*, 17 January 1981 (reprinted in V. Herman and J. Alt (eds), *Cabinet Studies: A Reader*. London: Macmillan, 1975, 210–20).

Jones, G. (1975) 'Development of the Cabinet', in W. Thornhill (ed.), *The Modernization of British Government*. London: Pitman.

Kaufman, G. (1981) *How to be a Minister*. London: Sidgwick and Jackson.

Kogan, M. (ed.) (1971) *The Politics of Education: Edward Boyle and Anthony Crosland in Conversation with Maurice Kogan*. Harmondsworth, Middlesex: Penguin.

Mackintosh, J. P. (1977) *The British Cabinet*, 3rd edn. London: Stevens.

Mitchie, A. and S. Hoggart (1978) *The Pact: The Inside Story of the Lib-Lab Government, 1977–8*. London: Quartet.

Morrison, H. (1954) *Government and Parliament: A View from the Inside*. Oxford: Oxford University Press.

Norton, P. (1980) *Dissension in the House of Commons, 1974–9*. Oxford: Oxford University Press.

Page, B. (1978) 'The Secret Constitution', *New Statesman*, 21 July 1978.

Pliatzky, L. (1981) *Getting and Spending: Public Expenditure, Employment and Inflation*. Oxford: Basil Blackwell.

Rose, R. (1971) 'The Making of Cabinet Ministers', *British Journal of Political Science*, 1: 393–414.

Rose, R. (1980) 'Government against Sub-Governments: a European Perspective', pp. 284–347 in R. Rose and E. Suleiman (eds), *Presidents and Prime Ministers*. Washington DC: American Enterprise Institute.

Rush, M. (1984) *The Cabinet and Policy Formation*. London: Longman.

Seldon, A. (1981) *Churchill's Indian Summer: The Conservative Government, 1951–55*. London: Hodder and Stoughton.

Seymour-Ure, C. (1971) 'The Disintegration of the Cabinet and the Neglected Question of Cabinet Reform', *Parliamentary Affairs*, 24: 196–207.

Seymour-Ure, C. (1984) 'British "War Cabinets" in Limited Wars: Korea, Suez and the Falklands', *Public Administration*, 62: 181–200.

Steel, D. (1980) *A House Divided: The Lib-Lab Pact and the Future of British Politics*. London: Weidenfeld and Nicolson.

Walker, P. Gordon (1972) *The Cabinet*, revised edn. Glasgow and London: Collins and Fontana.

Wilson, H. (1976) *The Governance of Britain*. London: Weidenfeld and Nicolson and Michael Joseph.

5
Cabinet committees in Canada: pressures and dysfunctions stemming from the representational imperative

Colin Campbell

5.1 Introduction

The federal government in Canada has developed one of the most elaborate systems available to aficionados of the institutionalization of specialized, cabinet-level deliberative bodies. This fact is no fluke of history. Canada has always been a highly segmented society. The exigencies of coherent rule have normally imposed upon government parties exaggerated discipline. Thus, regional and sectoral interests have found their most effective expression in secret negotiations between the leadership of contesting sectors and regions (Lijphart, 1977: 118–29; Matheson, 1976: 22–25; Punnett, 1977: 65–70). Public contestation on the part of competing members of the same caucus in the House of Commons simply exacerbates profound fears about the viability of a federal government which — in addition to being seriously segmented — must constantly give due obeisance its citizens' desire to do things differently from Americans. This is the one patriotic principle upon which virtually everyone agrees. A nation founded on such a negative aspiration provides the ideal environment in which government becomes a massive holding action.

Under these circumstances, attentive publics do not expect that the aggregation of their special pleading will occur up front, in the public forum. The paramountcy of national solidarity dictates that, above all else, the external image of internal harmony prevail. The segments of society that really count need not hear their particularistic claims publicly registered by members of the government party. When the system works, they know that their views have been brought to bear on the deliberations of the principal officers of the executive branch gathered in the cabinet or one of its committees. Cabinet, in this respect, serves as the effective representative body at the centre of government. Though its proceedings are secret, it must, in so far as possible, incorporate convincing spokesmen for all regional, linguistic, cultural and sectoral groups pivotal to maintenance of a government's mandate.

As will become clear in this chapter, a very strong trade off operates at the heart of the representational roles of cabinets. Cabinet's function as executive-branch omnibuses presents very serious dangers of overload. That is, the representational imperative places unrelenting upward pressures on the size of cabinets. While considerable load factors help appease numerous segments of society, the constraints upon government manageability raise questions about the dysfunctions of an excess of ministers and departments. Canada has developed its highly complex system of cabinet committees in an effort to overcome the diseconomies resulting from overly large cabinets. At the same time, it has preserved — even expanded — the representational character of the government of the day. This chapter will begin by reviewing institutionalization of cabinet-level bodies up to 1968 when Pierre Elliott Trudeau became prime minister. Subsequent sections will examine the organization and functions of cabinet committees during the Trudeau, Clark, Turner and Mulroney governments.

5.2 The evolution of an approach

Canada's cabinet is a purely conventional entity. That is, it receives no explicit mention in the Constitution Act (formerly the British North American Act, 1867). Indeed, not even the prime minister's role is specified in the written constitution. Two references to the prime minister in the Constitution Act of 1982 — containing the charter of rights and freedoms, and other measures — simply stipulate that he or she convene constitutional conferences including himself or herself and provincial premiers one and fifteen years after the act came into force.

Although it lacks a formally prescribed role, cabinet has enjoyed, since confederation, full legitimacy deriving from conventional practice. The preamble to the 1867 Constitution Act states simply that Canada will have a 'Constitution in Principle similar to that of the United Kingdom'. This seemingly vague provision effectively stipulated the observance by Canada of all conventional practices in effect in Britain in 1867 (Dawson, 1963: 18–9, 62–3). In fact, the provinces of British North America joining the new dominion already employed cabinet systems of government along the lines followed in the United Kingdom.

The representational function of cabinet derives to a significant degree from colonial antecedent. Most clearly, a convention of duality operated at the heart of the Union of Canada under which Quebec and Ontario had been jointly governed since 1840. Here each department had two ministers, one from Canada East (Quebec) and the other from Canada West (Ontario) (Morton, 1955: 113–25). As well, each cabinet consisted equally of ministers with French origins and those with British ancestry. In some respects, arrangements under the new dominion only intensified attention to representational criteria for cabinet membership. Totalling thirteen, the initial ministerial complement provided five positions for the most populous 'region' — namely Ontario — and four each for the other two — Quebec and Maritimes. The crafters of the first dominion cabinet attempted as well to assure that their selections gave due regard to the sectarian affiliations and the economic interests of ministers.

Ministers' numbers held fairly firm between the initial thirteen and a maximum of nineteen from 1867 to 1935. In fact, Mackenzie King's 1935 cabinet had only sixteen members. This did not mean that cabinet overload had not become a concern among observers. The intensity of the representational norm meant that cabinet frequently became bogged down in detail. As well, the proliferation of boards and commissions gave departments only a tenuous hold on much of the apparatus of state. In 1912, the Prime Minister, Sir Robert Borden, retained Sir George Murray, a former Permanent Secretary of the UK Treasury, to examine ways of improving the organization of the Canadian public service (Mallory, 1971: 103). Sir George's central recommendations set an agenda with which reforms on into our current decade still struggle:

> the devolution of more legal and administrative powers to individual ministers, thereby circumscribing the Canadian practice of collective cabinet responsibility; the grouping of administrative tasks under departments rather than the proliferating boards and commissions...; the adoption of an 'inner' and 'outer' cabinet; the creation of 'political deputy ministers' to relieve the ministers from many administrative tasks (Wilson, 1981: 329).

In 1917, Sir George's own government appointed him to the Haldane Committee which similarly sought ways to streamline cabinet government in the UK (Chapman and Greenway 1980: 78–82).

Multiple, specialized committees did not take shape in the Canadian system until the Second World War. However, one committee, the Treasury Board — which since 1869 has even claimed a statutory base — dates back to the very beginning of Confederation (Campbell and Szablowski, 1979: 29). With varying degrees of effective authority, this committee has, since its inception, attempted to maintain financial and managerial discipline in the government in so far as this can be accomplished without burdening the entire cabinet. Before the First World War, Britain attempted to convince the dominions of the need for defence committees to prepare for the impending 'war emergency' (Mallory, 1971: 105). It took Canada until 1917 actually to set up War, and Reconstruction and Development committees. Neither survived beyond 1918.

A standing Defense Committee did emerge in 1936. After the onslaught of the Second World War, the government adopted the committee approach wholesale. It had established ten cabinet-level bodies by the end of 1939. Here the 'War Committee' functioned, much like its counterparts in First and Second World War Britain, as a surrogate for full cabinet in directing the war effort (Heeney, 1946: 28; Mackintosh, 1977: 371–9, 490–9; Turner, 1980). Ad hoc mandates served as the basis for many other committees (Mallory, 1971: 106). Even those considered to be 'standing' functioned sporadically. This pattern continued through the postwar period until the mid 1960s. John Diefenbaker's government (1957–63) provides an exception here. The populist prime minister believed that the entire cabinet, not committees, should make his government's decisions. For instance, he convened the cabinet 164 times in 1959 as against Louis St Laurent's 91 meetings in 1956 (Newman, 1963: 93). Pearson — prime minister from 1963–8 — reinstated committees as instruments for easing the decision load of full cabinet. He also set in motion a rationalization of the cabinet system whereby committees would shoulder responsibility for broad areas of government activity (Robertson, 1971: 490). As we will see in section 5.3, Pierre Trudeau fashioned from Pearson's concept one of the most complex and institutionalized networks of cabinet committees in the world.

Simultaneous with the evolution of a routinized and specialized cabinet decision-making process, three parallel developments were reshaping the permanent bureaucracy's involvement at the highest levels of executive leadership. First, a convention began to take hold which allowed committees comprised of deputy ministers (i.e. the top civil servants) to 'shadow' cabinet-level groups (Granatstein, 1981: 86, 92, 145, 253, 332). In at least one such instance, the formation in 1949 of the Interdepartmental Committee on External Trade Policy which prepared issues for the Cabinet Committee on Economic Policy, a deputies' body began to assume coordinative functions taking in virtually the entire compass of government (Granatstein, 1981: 253).

Second, the officer responsible since 1867 for recording cabinet actions, the clerk of the Privy Council, received the additional title of Secretary to the Cabinet in 1940. The new nomenclature formalized the intensification of the Privy Council Office's (PCO) functioning as a cabinet secretariat. Under the aegis of its mandate to bring greater order to the flow of cabinet business, PCO began to weigh in heavily on matters concerning the formation and composition of cabinet-level and official committees, and even to chair some sub-cabinet bodies (Heeney, 1946; Granatstein, 1981 and 1982). Thus began the central agency's custodial concern for the interdepartmental decision-making apparatus.

Finally, deputy ministers and less senior officials with salient expertise began to gain access to meetings of cabinet and its committees in the 1940s (Granatstein, 1982: 207). The prevailing norms of Whitehall still frown upon this level of participation in the principal forums of executive politics (see 4.3). With one party's control of the federal government for an overwhelming proportion of the past fifty years, Canadian permanent bureaucrats' direct involvement with cabinet-level deliberations led to considerable cross-fertilization between the folkways and agendas of the public service and Liberal ministries (Campbell and Szablowski, 1979: 153–62).

5.3 Trudeau: 1968–79

Pierre Trudeau pursued with exceptional rigour efforts to rationalize cabinet's management of its business. In part, he focused on imposition of very strict order in the timing and form of departmental submissions to cabinet and its committees (French, 1979). Additionally, his strong interest in comprehensive planning enshrined as a central principle to interdepartmental dynamics a belief in the advantages to breaking cabinet decision-making into manageable issue areas. This would override the dysfunctions stemming from Canada's relatively large number of portfolios (Pitfield, 1976; Szablowski, 1977; Dobuzinskis, 1977). For the first time, cabinet began routinely to accept the guidance of committees as not requiring further deliberation if dissenting ministers failed to notify formally the PCO of their objections (Mallory, 1971: 107).

The comprehensive bent of Trudeau's system stemmed largely from overarching committees responsible for giving direction to and reviewing the deliberations of sectoral committees. Here Priorities and Planning operated as the steering group for coordinating the cabinet decisions process, reviews within specialized committees, and the policy stances and activities of departments; Federal-Provincial examined all matters with major intergovernmental implications; the Treasury Board ruled on the physical and human resources available for various programmes, and it developed and enforced government-wide administration policies; and Legislation and House Planning performed ringmaster functions connected with obtaining from Parliament any requisite acts and resolutions.

The composition of cabinet committees was secret until 1979. However, Campbell and Szablowski (1979: 154–5) derived the 1978 distribution of cabinet portfolios under the policy sectors from in-depth interview materials. The accuracy of their results was verified by members of PCO who would not go on record. Table 5.1 summarizes the findings. Nine portfolios came under Economic Policy, seven under Social Policy, six under External and Defence Policy, five under Culture and Native Affairs, and seven under Government Operations. In the cases of the departments of Finance, Industry, Trade and Commerce, Agriculture, and Labor, the programme associated with portfolios overlapped committee jurisdictions. This fact drives home the difficulty of dividing government into watertight sectors. It combines with the number of portfolios to, in some cases, cancel out the advantages to specialized decision groups in a very large cabinet. That is, some sectoral committees got very large and unwieldy.

Two other factors exacerbated these circumstances. First, some ministers occupied such central positions in cabinet that they enjoyed the right to attend all cabinet committees at any time or even to send an official to represent them. In 1978, these included the finance minister, the president of the Treasury Board, and the deputy prime minister and president of the Privy Council. Second, any ministers vitally concerned with a specific matter before a committee other than the one under which their portfolio fell could exercise their right to attend any policy sector meeting on an ad hoc basis.

Interestingly, not every policy committee had a fixed chair. That is, the nature of agenda items determined which of two potential lead ministers would chair three of the five committees. Social Policy alternated between the ministers of national health and welfare, and the minister of justice; External and Defense between the secretary of state for external affairs and the minister of defense; and Culture and Native Affairs between the secretary of state and the minister of indian affairs and northern development. Further, membership on Priorities and Planning — clearly the most senior panel — followed, in so far as Campbell and Szablowski (1979) could ascertain, representational criteria somewhat independent of lead roles on sectoral committees. To be sure, the prime minister, the deputy prime minister, the finance minister, and the president of the Treasury Board, all sat on Priorities and Planning. However, the ministers of national defense, indian affairs and northern development did not — at least on a regular basis. On the other

TABLE 5.1

Policy sectors, lead ministers, and departments within sectors

Policy sector	Lead minister(s) within the sector	Departments within sectors
Economic	Minister of Finance	Finance; Regional Economic Expansion; Industry, Trade and Commerce; National Revenue; Energy, Mines and Resources; Agriculture; Consumer and Corporate Affairs; Fisheries; Small Business
Social	Minister of National Health & Welfare or Minister of Justice (depending on issue)	Health and Welfare; Justice; Labor; Urban Affairs; Employment and Immigration; Solicitor General; Veterans' Affairs
External and Defence	Secretary of State for External Affairs or Minister of National Defence (depending on issue)	External Affairs; Defence; CIDA; Industry, Trade and Commerce (international trade); Labor (ILO); Finance (IMF, GATT, OECD)
Culture and Native Affairs	Secretary of State or Minister of Indian Affairs and Northern Development (depending on issue)	Secretary of State; Indian Affairs and Northern Development; Communications; Fitness and Amateur Sport; Multiculturalism
Government Operations	Minister of Transport	Transport; Environment; Public Works; Supply and Services; Science and Technology; Post Office; Agriculture

Source: Campbell and Szablowski (1979: 154–5).

hand, the minister of labor did. No doubt, some efforts to achieve fairly even regional apportionment and to give due prominence to ministers especially important to the political fortunes of the government played a significant role in Trudeau's assignment of colleagues to Priorities and Planning.

As the reader no doubt anticipates, Canada's elaborate and highly routinized committee system requires very complex arrangements for routing cabinet work through the chain of collective executive authority. At each level, either free-standing central agencies or PCO secretariats provide staff support. Figure 5.1

FIGURE 5.1
Executive leadership in Canada under Pierre Elliott Trudeau, 1979

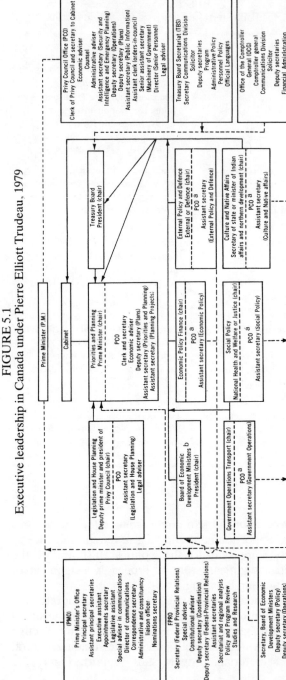

Notes: [a] Reporting to deputy secretary (Operations), PCO.

[b] Shadowed by a committee of senior officials, including the deputy ministers of member departments plus the clerk of the Privy Council, the secretary to the Cabinet, and the assistant secretary of the Economic Policy Committee, and chaired by the secretary of the Board of Economic Development Ministers.

[c] Member departments generate proposals; those with expenditure implications are reviewed by Priorities and Planning before going to the Cabinet.

Source: Campbell (1980: 57).

portrays the various committees, offices and reporting lines during the final year of Trudeau's first mandate. To the five sectoral committees found in Table 5.1, the prime minister added late in 1978 the Board of Economic Development Ministers. In the aftermath of the Quebec separatists' election victory in November 1976, Priorities and Planning's absorption with federal-provincial relations made a separate coordinative committee working in that field redundant.

When an item of business entered the collective process, the PCO would assign it to the relevant sectoral committee. Through a 1976 agreement reached between PCO and the Treasury Board Secretariat (TBS), the latter could request at this point to review the expenditure implications of any submission. Previously, TBS — unless departments voluntarily consulted it at an earlier point — had to wait until cabinet documents cleared the relevant committee to review the merits of a proposal and make a recommendation to cabinet. Whatever, all measures with significant expenditure implications would have to win separate approval by the Treasury Board. The nature of Priorities and Planning's role regarding issues coming through the process varied greatly according to their importance. A hidden-hand Priorities and Planning function worked its effect on virtually all business. The committee, after all, exerted ultimate authority over the development of the directives for departments on the policy priorities in effect for annual legislative calendars and the broad expenditure guidelines in force for fiscal years. In addition, the committee would frequently fill its agenda with issues which, though central to the government's plans, proved difficult to resolve in sectoral committees because of their magnitude, political volatility or both.

The period covered by Figure 5.1 represents one of ferment for central agencies and the secretariats supporting cabinet and its committees. By 1975, the Federal-Provincial Relations Office (FPRO) had spun off from PCO. As the government grappled with the separatist threat in Quebec and efforts to revamp the constitution, FPRO expanded into a full-fledged central agency. In 1976, the last straw in a succession of crushing auditor general's reports forced the government into a grand gesture to assuage public fears over financial management. Trudeau created an Office of the Comptroller General which would operate under the highest deputy-minister level in tandem with the Treasury Board Secretariat. The new agency, in addition to improving departmental monitoring of expenditure, would furnish the Treasury Board with data from effectiveness and efficiency evaluations of government programmes.

Finally, and most significantly, the Board of Economic Development Ministers became the only sectoral committee with its very own central agency when it was created late in 1978. For public consumption, a breakdown of negotiations with business and labor over industrial policy along with a stampede of departments after $300 million added funds for economic development in the midst of an austerity programme provided the rationale for this extraordinary move (Campbell, 1983: 194). In fact, PCO, long disturbed by its ongoing conflict with the Treasury Board Secretariat over resource allocations, came up with the idea that sectoral committees should exert discretion over conflicting claims upon resources within broad 'envelopes' of expenditure (Van Loon, 1981).

5.4 The Clark debacle

Joe Clark took a wrong turn after becoming prime minister in May 1979. As head of a minority government, he should have recognized that he did not have much time to make his mark before returning to the polls for a stronger mandate. He should have convened Parliament right away in order to introduce at least some of his legislative agenda before his honeymoon began to wear off. Instead, Clark waited almost five months to call Parliament into session. By that time, even the Progressive Conservative faithful began to view him as a 'do nothing' prime minister.

To this day, high-ranking Progressive Conservatives maintain that the Clark government did not err by delaying the opening of Parliament. As the conventional wisdom goes, the fact that the party had not served as the government for sixteen years meant that every minister faced an exceptionally sharp 'learning curve.' The herd instinct was to hunker down and 'learn' how each department worked.

This frame of mind provided the ideal soil for PCO's designs for the new government. It offered an interregnum in which the permanent bureaucracy's institutional engineers could roll out their blueprints for the brave new apparatus of state and actually retain the attention of ministers. The government members found themselves strapped to their desks pouring over briefing books, not just about their departments, but about how the entire cabinet decision process should be reorganized as well.

Under the system adopted during Summer 1979, Priorities and Planning was restyled the 'Inner Cabinet.' In some respects, the new nomenclature simply ratified Priorities and Planning's role as the executive committee of cabinet. However, the fact that Clark rarely convened full cabinet gave added force to the committee's preeminence. The new government cut the number of sectoral committees to four. Two committees — Economic Development, and Social and Native Affairs — would call upon the support of their own central agencies, respectively, the ministries of state for 'Economic' and 'Social' development. The Federal-Provincial Relations Committee was reinstituted. As well, a Communications Committee took on the dual task of following through on Clark's open government election pledges and improving the coordination of the bureaucracy's public information offices.

Relatedly, the new government made public the membership as well as structure of the cabinet committee system. Thus, some bodies which normally met irregularly and rarely attracted much notice — even among attentive commentators — took fixed places on observers' radar scopes. These are the Special Committee of Council which reviews routine orders-in-council, Security and Intelligence which coordinates intelligence concerning both internal and external security, Labor Relations which manages crises brought on by industrial disputes, and Public Service which monitors the development and implementation of policies concerning the career bureaucracy.

In addition to accepting these alterations to the committee system, the Clark government adopted across all expenditure fields PCO's belief that sectoral committees, rather than the Treasury Board, should rule upon the allocation of resources to specific programmes. Dubbed the 'envelope system,' the new arrangement apportioned programmes within nine umbrella categories to the four sectoral committees and the Inner Cabinet. The latter body shouldered responsibility for fiscal arrangements with provinces, local governments and utilities, and management of the public debt. Even on the conceptual level the system is flawed. We will look more closely at why in section 5.5. Yet, notwithstanding the conceivable merits of the envelope approach, the minority government of a party that had not been in power for sixteen years simply should not have launched upon such a sweeping reform.

A look at Table 5.2 suggests the degree to which committee responsibilities tax ministers. Under Clark, both Inner Cabinet and Outer Cabinet members — the latter excluding ministers of state — held, on average, approximately 4.6 committee assignments. In a system so oriented to representational criteria for committee membership, it stands to reason that rank-and-file ministers responsible for operational departments might carry roughly the same burden of committee work as those with more sharply defined coordinative roles. Clark's ministers, thus, faced a formidable enough task in developing the requisite routines and folkways for operating effectively in such a highly articulated cabinet committee system. By taking on the further task of 'shaking down' PCO's envelope concept, the new government simply exceeded its capacity to learn.

5.5 Trudeau's return

It was not by coincidence that on his return to office in July 1980 Trudeau altered very little the reforms of the cabinet committee system introduced under Clark. His reinstatement of Michael Pitfield, the clerk of the Privy Council and secretary to the cabinet whom Clark had deposed for being too strongly associated with Trudeau, spoke volumes. The organizational engineer who had spawned the envelope idea was back at his perch at the very top of the permanent bureaucracy. And, as always, he enjoyed the implicit trust of the prime minister.

Trudeau did demote the 'Inner Cabinet' back down to 'Priorities and Planning.' As well, his cabinet met virtually every week. Still, Priorities and Planning functioned essentially as the executive committee of cabinet. It also recaptured the lead for the federal-provincial relations from the committee by that name which once again became defunct. Separatist rumblings in Western Canada coupled with the fact that the new government claimed only two MPs west of Ontario led to establishment of a Western Affairs committee. However, even secondment of three ministers from the Senate — an appointive body — only allowed for four of thirteen members of the committee who actually hailed from the West.

Interestingly, the distribution of committee memberships under Trudeau as reflected in Table 5.3 resulted in a sharp distinction between members of Priorities and Planning and the rest of the cabinet — excluding once again ministers of state. The average Priorities and Planning minister had 5.3 positions while the others had only 3.8. This tack eased the burden of committee work for several heads of operational departments. It also increased the relative weight of Priorities and Planning members on all committees. When we take into account the Canadian convention whereby ministers might delegate officials to represent them in committees, it became clear that ministers outside the charmed circle frequently would have to justify their programmes or policy proposals before mixed groups. These would include some members of Priorities and Planning, fellow supplicant ministers and the permanent civil service surrogates for senior colleagues who were just too busy to attend meetings in person.

A renewed emphasis on 'shadow' meetings of deputies paralleled Priorities and Planning ministers' or their career surrogates'

TABLE 5.2
Clark government, October 1979

(a) *Inner Cabinet*

Ministers			Position	Province
1.	Clark	(2)	Prime Minister	Alberta
2.	Flynn (Senator)	(6)	Leader of Senate; Justice	Quebec
4.	Baker	(8)	President of Privy Council House Leader; Revenue	Ontario
5.	MacDonald (F)	(4)	External Affairs	Ontario
9.	Crosbie	(6)	Finance	Newfoundland
10.	MacDonald (D)	(5)	Secretary of State; Communication	Prince Edward Island
12.	LaSalle	(5)	Supply & Services	Quebec
17.	Jarvis	(3)	Federal-Provincial Relations	Ontario
19.	Stevens	(4)	President of Treasury Board	Ontario
22.	Hnatyshyn	(3)	Energy, Mines and Resources	Saskatchewan
24.	de Cotret (Senator)	(3)	Industry, Trade & Commerce; Economic Development	
16.	Fraser	(6)	Post Office; Environment	British Columbia

(b) *Cabinet Committees*

Sectoral	Chairman	Coordinative	Chairman
Economic Development	de Cotret	Treasury Board	Stevens
Foreign & Defence Policy	MacDonald (F)	Legislation and	
Social & Native Affairs	MacDonald (D)	House Planning	Baker
Economy in Government	Stevens	F-P Relations	Jarvis

Other	Chair
Special Committee of Council	Baker
Security and Intelligence	Clark
Labor Relations	Neilsen (Yukon)
Public Service	Clark
Communications	Baker

(c) *Outer Cabinet*

Ministers			Position	Province
6.	McGrath	(4)	Fisheries and Oceans	Newfoundland
7.	Neilsen	(4)	Public Works	Yukon
8.	Lawrence	(6)	Solicitor General; Consumer and Corporate Affairs	Ontario
11.	Alexander	(5)	Labor	Ontario
13.	Mazankowski	(6)	Transport; Wheat Board	Alberta
14.	MacKay	(6)	Regional and Economic Expansion; Central Mortgage and Housing	Nova Scotia
15.	Epp	(4)	Indian Affairs and Northern Development	Manitoba
18.	McKinnon	(5)	Defense; Veterans Affairs	British Columbia
20.	Wise	(4)	Agriculture	Ontario
21.	Atkey	(6)	Employment and Immigration	Ontario
23.	Crombie	(5)	Health and Welfare	Ontario
25.	Grafftey	(1)	Science and Technology	Quebec

(d) *Ministers of State*

Ministers			Position	Province
3.	Asselin (Senator)	—	Canadian International Development Agency	Quebec
26.	Beattie	(1)	Treasury Board	Ontario
27.	Howie	(2)	Transport	New Brunswick
28.	Paproski	—	Fitness and Amateur Sport; Multiculturalism	Alberta
29.	Huntington	(1)	Small Business and Industry	British Columbia
30.	Wilson	(1)	International Trade	Ontario

Notes: Numbers indicate order of precedence after the Prime Minister. Numbers in parentheses denote membership of cabinet committees.

pervasive influence in all other committees. As noted above, shadow committees played prominent roles in the 1940s and 1950s as the institutionalization of cabinet-level bodies began to take shape. However, the practice waned as cabinet committees became more routinized. Increasingly, various task forces involving officials short of deputy minister rank prepared issues for cabinet review. These did not preclude deputies' groups. However, deputies tended mainly to interact in ad hoc meetings designed to break log jams over specific matters.

The first signs of a return to more formalized deputies' groups appeared in 1975. At the time, the Trudeau government was wrestling with conflicts within the bureaucracy over how to respond to stagflation. As it inched toward its eventual imposition of mandatory wage and price controls, a group of five deputy ministers called DM-5 began to function as the steering group for hammering out differences over the government's anti-inflation strategy. Once Trudeau adopted a mandatory programme, a broader group, DM-10, assumed the task of coordinating the implementation of controls. The next major initiative in the economics field, the 1978 creation of the Board of Economic Development Ministers, also saw the utilization of a shadow deputies' committee.

The 1980–4 Trudeau government brought on a full blossoming of the shadow system. At the very centre, the Coordinating Committee of Deputy Ministers (CCDM), chaired by the clerk of the Privy Council and the secretary to the cabinet, included the deputy heads of the Finance Department, the Treasury Board Secretariat, the Office of Comptroller General, the ministries of state for Economic Development and Social Development, and the Department of External Affairs. Apart from the fact that it excluded deputies whose ministers did not head central agencies or chair sectoral committees, CCDM shadowed Priorities and Planning. Mirror deputies' groups related similarly to each sectoral committee, with the exception that the deputy of each member minister belonged to the respective shadow groups. One such body, the Committee of Deputy Ministers on Foreign and Defense Policy, even maintained a separate secretariat housed in the Department of External Affairs to support its work.

Full implementation of the envelope approach, formally known as PEMS for 'Policy and Expenditure Management System', functioned as the driving force behind the elaborate innovations that took place under both Trudeau and Clark beginning in 1978. We should, thus, briefly examine the rationale and results of the system. PEMS attempted to ameliorate the conflicts between the Privy Council Office and the Treasury Board Secretariat over

TABLE 5.3
Trudeau government, July 1980

(a) *Priorities and Planning*

Ministers			Position	Province
1.	Trudeau	(3)	Prime Minister	Quebec
2.	MacEchen	(9)	Finance; Deputy Prime Minister	Nova Scotia
4.	Chretien	(6)	Justice; Social Development	Quebec
6.	Olson (Senator)	(5)	Economic Development	Alberta
8.	Gray	(4)	Industry, Trade and Commerce	Ontario
11.	Lalonde	(4)	Energy, Mines and Resources	Quebec
13.	LeBlanc	(6)	Fisheries and Oceans	New Brunswick
22.	MacGuigan	(3)	External Affairs	Ontario
24.	Fleming	(4)	Multiculturalism	Ontario
29.	Pinard	(7)	President of Privy Council	Quebec
30.	Johnston	(8)	President of Treasury Board	Quebec
31.	Axworthy	(5)	Employment and Immigration	Manitoba

(b) *Cabinet Committees*

Sectoral	Chairman	Coordinative	Chairman
Economic Development	Olson	Priorities & Planning	Trudeau
Foreign & Defense	MacGuigan	Treasury Board	Johnston
Government Operations	Pinard	Legislation and House	Pinard
Social Development	Chretien	Planning	

Other	Chair
Communications	Fleming
Labor Relations	Regan (Nova Scotia)
Public Service	Trudeau
Security and Intelligence	Trudeau
Special Committee of Council	Pinard
Western Affairs	Axworthy

(c) *Other Ministers*

Ministers			Position	Province
3.	Pepin	(6)	Transport	Quebec
5.	Munro	(4)	Indian Affairs and Northern Development	Ontario
7.	Whealan	(4)	Agriculture	Ontario
9.	Quellet	(5)	Consumer and Corporate Affairs; Postmaster General	Quebec
10.	MacDonald	(2)	Veterans Affairs	Prince Edward Island
12.	Perrault (Senator)	(5)	Government Leader in Senate	British Columbia
14.	Roberts	(5)	Science and Technology; Environment	Ontario
15.	Begin	(2)	Health and Welfare	Quebec
16.	Blais	(4)	Supply and Services	Ontario
17.	Fox	(4)	Secretary of State;	Quebec
18.	Lamontagne	(3)	Defense	Quebec
19.	De Bane	(3)	Regional Economic Expansion	Quebec
21.	Regan	(3)	Labor; Sports	Nova Scotia
23.	Kaplan	(4)	Solicitor General	Ontario
25.	Rompkey	(4)	Revenue	Newfoundland
32.	Cosgrove	(3)	Public Works	Ontario

(d) *Ministers of State*

20.	Argue (Senator)	(5)	Wheat Board	Saskatchewan
26.	Bussieres	(2)	Finance	Quebec
27.	Lapointe	(3)	Small Business	Quebec
28.	Lumely	(2)	Trade	Ontario
33.	Erola	(3)	Mines	Ontario

Notes: Numbers by names indicate order of precedence. Numbers in parentheses denote memberships on cabinet committees.

development of annual expenditure guidelines and the meshing of these with various government policies. It sought, in essence, to integrate cabinet consideration of policy and expenditure issues. The method had two elements. The first did not relate directly to the enhancement of the cabinet committee structure. It centred on inclusion of four future years in the annual fiscal plan in order to improve forward planning in policy and expenditure review. The second relied entirely on the more highly articulated machinery. It attempted to get ministers to plan along sectoral lines and not just according to individual departmental initiatives and appeals for a larger share of the expenditure pie.

The thinking behind the envelope system takes us into game theory too esoteric to probe deeply here (Campbell, 1983: 194–200). If ministers related to one another in more sharply delineated and highly routinized policy sectors, the resulting collective sense would moderate their instincts toward empire-building. Capped by the provision that newly freed funds would stay in each sector, the resulting 'communities of interest' would encourage ministers to identify potential savings in their own departments. Such altruism would stem from improved budgetary odds. Rather than reverting to the general fund, freed money would remain in its original envelope. Thus, the minister offering up a sacrificial sum could put in a bid for its return to his department, albeit for a truly deserving programme. Think of how willingly Abraham would have taken Isaac to the altar of sacrifice if he knew all along that God was just kidding and that he even stood a chance of receiving a choicer remit!

As some might expect, the envelope system has run less than satisfactorily. In fiscal year 1982–3, the federal government's expenditures exceeded revenues by fully 50 per cent. For 1983–4, the 7.1 per cent of GNP taken by the deficit more than doubled the 3.2 comparable figure for the United Kingdom. Such statistics indicate the degree to which ministerial communities of interest failed to check runaway spending. As well, the literature abounds with evidence of very poorly handled sectoral policy initiatives and decisions. The outstanding cases include the largely abortive yet extremely costly effort to launch petroleum mega-projects (Doern, 1983); the immense fiscal strains brought on by the grandiose effort to revamp taxation, investment and ownership in the petroleum sector (Doern, 1984); Trudeau's last government's failure through the recession of the early 1980s to trim social programmes except through arbitrary administration of a budgetary cleaver (Prince, 1984); and, notwithstanding the fanfare, the near total inability of ministers concerned with regional and economic development to produce a coherent industrial policy (Lithwick and Devlin, 1984).

5.6 **The Turner interlude**

By the time that John Turner became prime minister on 30 June, 1984 after Trudeau's resignation as Liberal leader, he had spent nearly nine years out of government. Thus, he had missed entirely the institutional ferment connected with implementation of the envelope system. As well, like many other observers, he had come to the conclusion that the immense organizational dislocation resulting from PEMS more than negated any benefits from the approach. In a press conference held after he took power, Turner explicitly distanced himself from Trudeau's system of cabinet government which he described as 'too elaborate, too complex, too slow and too expensive.' He added that the highly intricate processes introduced by Trudeau had 'diffused and eroded and blurred' the authority of cabinet ministers. This strong critique from a fellow Liberal only makes sense in light of the fact Turner had left government in 1975 after a major rift with Trudeau.

Turner acted decisively to abandon central elements of Trudeau's infrastructure. He cut the size of cabinet from thirty-seven ministers to twenty-nine. He reduced the number of cabinet committees from thirteen to ten. This move eliminated 'Communications', 'Labor Relations', and 'Western Affairs'. He abolished the ministries of state for Economic and Regional Development and Social Development. While not dismantling entirely the PEMS system, he took steps aimed at streamlining cabinet decision-making. These included clarification of ministers' authority over their departments, control of the number of items reaching cabinet, limiting submissions to the Treasury Board, discontinuing central agency 'assessment notes' appended to cabinet's basic decision documents which take the form of executive summary, and curtailing the role of 'mirror' deputies' committees and the access of officials to meetings of cabinet and its committees. Of course, the Liberals' immediate absorption by a general election resulting in their ousting by September meant that Turner never actually seized control of the apparatus of state. Thus, his scaled-down cabinet system never was tested out.

5.7 **Mulroney**

Brian Mulroney departed from Turner's reforms in only one substantial way: in a clear reversal of Turner's tack, Mulroney assembled the largest cabinet in history — consisting of forty ministers. In other respects, Mulroney's innovations followed along the lines of Turner's changes. First, he eliminated the cabinet committee of Foreign and Defense Policy. He reduced the number of expenditure envelopes by merging 'Energy' with 'Economic and

Regional Development', and 'Justice and Legal Affairs' with 'Social Affairs'. This meant that the two main domestic sectoral committees consolidated their domains into one envelope each. Finally, he gave Priorities and Planning responsibility for the 'External Affairs and Aid' and 'Defense' envelopes. Priorities and Planning thus gained jurisdiction over a portion of the entire federal budget second only to the Social Development Committee's. In view of the former committee's overall responsibility for establishing the broad policy and expenditure guidelines for the PEMS system, the burden of direct and detailed responsibility for two envelopes in addition to the pair — 'Fiscal Transfers' and 'Public Debt' — already held presents serious dangers of overload.

One arrangement under Mulroney could potentially alter the role of the prime minister within the entire collective decision-making apparatus. Mulroney imparted to his deputy prime minister a host of responsibilities, some of which had never been held by a predecessor, specifically oriented to cabinet business. The beneficiary, Erik Nielsen, took on, thus, the vice-chairmanships of Priorities and Planning and cabinet, chairmanship of the Special Committee of Council, ex-officio memberships on all sectoral committees, and responsibility for government communications. Perhaps most important, Nielsen would chair a ministerial task force consisting of the president of the Treasury Board, and the finance and justice ministers. This body launched on an elaborate examination of each portfolio with a view to consolidating departmental programmes, regulations and delivery mechanisms. A special staff under the secretary to the Treasury Board would support the Nielsen task force. In other words, the deputy prime minister obtained a mission to flush out waste, duplication and outdated government activities with three of his most senior colleagues and the requisite secretariat.

Such a mandate to a deputy prime minister raises question about Mulroney's motives and intent. When we consider that Nielsen held under the Clark government the relatively obscure Public Works portfolio and did not belong to Priorities and Planning, a look into why his fortunes proved so different under Mulroney becomes compelling. A surge of characteristic magnanimity when Mulroney became leader of the party in 1983 had preordained a special role for Nielsen. Joe Clark's bid to remain at the Progressive Conservative helm in 1982 necessitated the appointment of Nielsen, then house leader and a consummate parliamentary strategist, as interim national leader from February to June 1983. Nielsen, a Clark supporter, even registered qualms about Mulroney at the end of the party convention when he introduced him as 'not his first choice,

TABLE 5.4
Mulroney government, September 1984

(a) *Priorities and Planning*

Ministers			Position	Province
1.	Mulroney	(3)	Prime Minister	Quebec
4.	Clark	(3)	External Affairs	Alberta
5.	MacDonald	(5)	Employment and Immigration	Ontario
6.	Nielsen	(8)	Deputy Prime Minister; President of Privy Council	Yukon
7.	Crosbie	(6)	Justice	Newfoundland
9.	Mazankowski	(2)	Transport	Alberta
11.	Epp	(2)	Health and Welfare	Manitoba
12.	Fraser	(3)	Fisheries and Oceans	British Columbia
13.	Stevens	(2)	Regional Industrial Expansion	Ontario
15.	Hnatyshyn	(5)	Government House Leader	Saskatchewan
17.	de Cotret	(6)	President of Treasury Board	Quebec
19.	Wilson	(8)	Finance	Ontario
20.	Coates	(4)	Defense	Nova Scotia
29.	Carney	(2)	Energy, Mines and Resources	British Columbia
37.	Masse	(3)	Communications	Quebec

(b) *Cabinet Committees*

Sectoral	Chairman	Coordinative	Chairman
Economic and Regional Development	Stevens	Priorities and Planning	Mulroney
		Ministerial Task Force	Nielsen
Government Operations	de Cotret	Treasury Board	de Cotret
Social Development	Epp	Legislation & House Planning	Hnatyshyn

Other	Chair
Public Service	Mulroney
Security and Intelligence	Mulroney
Special Committee of Council	Nielsen

(c) *Other Ministers*

Ministers			Position	Province
2.	Hees	(3)	Veterans Affairs	Ontario
3.	Roblin (Senator)	(3)	Senate Government Leader	New Brunswick
8.	LaSalle	(2)	Public Works	Quebec
10.	MacKay	(4)	Solicitor General	Nova Scotia
14.	Wise	(2)	Agriculture	Ontario
16.	Crombie	(2)	Indian Affairs and Northern Development	Ontario
18.	Beatty	(3)	Revenue	Ontario
22.	Andre	(1)	Supply and Services	Alberta
24.	Siddon	(2)	Science and Technology	British Columbia
26.	McKnight	(4)	Labor	Saskatchewan
27.	McLean	(3)	Secretary of State	Ontario
31.	Blais-Grenier	(2)	Environment	Quebec
34.	Cote	(3)	Consumer & Corporate Affairs	Quebec

(d) *Ministers of State*

Ministers			Position	Province
23.	Jelinek	(2)	Fitness and Amateur Sport	Ontario
25.	Mayer	(1)	Wheat Board	Manitoba
28.	McMillan	(1)	Tourism	Prince Edward Island
30.	Bissonnette	(3)	Small Business	Quebec
32.	Bouchard	(2)	Transport	Quebec
33.	Champagne	(2)	Youth	Quebec
35.	Kelleher	(2)	International Trade	Ontario
36.	Layton	(2)	Mines	Quebec
38.	McDougall	(2)	Finance	Ontario
39.	Merrithew	(4)	Forestry	New Brunswick
40.	Vezina	(3)	External Relations	Quebec

Notes: Numbers by names indicate order of precedence. Numbers in parentheses denote memberships on cabinet committees.

but the new leader'. In a stroke which only history can deem brilliant or foolish, Mulroney retorted that Nielsen was his first choice as house leader. Eventually, Nielsen functioned formally as deputy national leader. His responsibilities included overseeing shadow cabinet operations. Mulroney simply does not like meetings. Further, he functioned poorly when he chaired shadow cabinet proceedings. He leaned heavily upon Nielsen to fill the breach.

Mulroney privately acknowledged his likely limitations as an effective director of cabinet dynamics. This fact, along with the understanding that Nielsen's special role in the official opposition would carry over to the new government, raised very high expectations for the deputy party leader among his supporters on the Progressive Conservative transition team. In fact, the final briefing material from this body asserted that Nielsen should chair all sectoral committees. This amounted to the Nielsen group pushing their man too hard by half. However, Mulroney's final formulation of his deputy's role reflects an amicable compromise. Nielsen functions as the prime minister's surrogate in many sessions of committees that the latter formally chairs, keeps a hand in all sectoral committees without carrying direct charge for their operation, and runs a supergrade committee. Of course, the latter enjoys the widest possible opening for pressing the nostrums of his cabinet colleagues who believe that government is far too big and expensive.

Table 5.4 reveals that, of the three governments that we have examined closely — Clarke's (1979–80), Trudeau's (1980–4) and Mulroney's — the latter introduced the highest degree of cabinet stratification. While the fifteen member Priorities and Planning Committee is relatively large, fully eleven members of cabinet rated only as ministers of state. Whereas the members of Priorities and Planning occupied, on average, 4.1 committee positions, other ministers and ministers of state filled, respectively, only 2.6 and 2.1 slots on cabinet-level bodies.

5.8 A final note on representation

Table 5.5 summarizes the distribution of cabinet positions under the Clark, Trudeau (1980–4) and Mulroney governments according to region. Under the former two governments, the thinness of caucus contingents from, respectively, Quebec and the West left cabinet with very uneven representativeness. In both instances, the prime minister dipped into the appointive Senate to bolster the contingent from the region in question. Clark appointed two senators representing Quebec and an additional Quebecois whom he had named to the upper house through an Ontario vacancy. This arrangement still left Clark with only five ministers from Canada's second most populous and overwhelmingly French-speaking province. Further, the two MPs topping off the meager Quebec complement ranged from a mediocre to poor in ability. Damage limitation dictated that the first of these take responsibility for 'Supply and Services' and the second 'Science and Technology'. Yet, the former minister gained entry to the Inner Cabinet as the candidate least likely to embarrass the government egregiously.

Trudeau faced a problem similar to Clark's with Quebec in providing representation from Western Canada. The Liberals only won two seats west of Ontario in the 1980 general election. The prime minister entrusted only one MP from the West, Lloyd Axworthy from Winnipeg, Manitoba, with a cabinet post. Senators filled the three remaining positions in the four-man Western group. One of these occupied the chairmanship of the Economic Development Committee. This senator and Axworthy, the latter by virtue of his chairmanship of 'Western Affairs', sat on Priorities and Planning.

The size and regional evenness of Mulroney's government caucus have spared him the balancing act faced by Clark and Trudeau. The leader of the government in the Senate is the only member of cabinet from the upper house. He has no departmental responsibilities. Nor does he sit on Priorities and Planning. Notwithstanding the

TABLE 5.5
Distribution of positions according to region

Government	Atlantic	Quebec	Ontario	West	Total
Clark					
Cabinet	5	4(2)	12(1)	9	30(3)
Inner Cabinet	2	2(1)	5(1)	3	12(2)
All Committee Posts	23	12(11)	50(3)	31	116(14)
Trudeau					
Cabinet	5	13	11	4(3)	33(3)
Priorities and					
Planning	2	5	3	2(1)	12(1)
All Committee Posts	24	56	40	20(15)	140(15)
Mulroney					
Cabinet	6(1)	11	11	12	40(1)
Priorities and					
Planning	2	3	3	7	15
All Committee Posts	22(3)	31	34	33	120(3)

Note: Figures in parentheses indicate number of posts held by senators.

relative regional balance in cabinet memberships and the distribution of committee posts, Quebec and Ontario claim only three representatives in Priorities and Planning as against the West's seven. The Quebec figure probably reflects the fact that MPs from that province mostly have no previous experience in Parliament, let alone cabinet. That five of the eleven ministers of state are from the province further suggests that Mulroney decided to ease his fellow Quebecois gradually into major cabinet roles. By the same token, the large Western contingent corresponds with the longevity of uninterrupted Parliamentary careers among Progressive Conservative MPs from that region of the country and their substantial numbers in the Clark government. While Ontario MPs were well-represented under Clark, they have not enjoyed career stability to the degree that the Westerners have.

5.9 Conclusion

Canada had established a system of specialized, standing cabinet committees by the Second World War. At the outset, the country largely took cues from parallel developments in the United Kingdom. However, representational pressures stemming from Canada's diversity began to add an element of urgency to the usual instrumental advantages of cabinet committees by the 1960s. Both Lester B. Pearson and Pierre Trudeau took measures designed to rationalize greatly the committee structure. Under each prime minister, the Privy Council Office solidified its role as the cabinet secretariat. This included a custodial interest in committees' capacity for reducing and channeling conflicts between cabinet members.

Through the late 1970s and early 1980s, two factors came together to intensify even further pressures to rationalize the cabinet committee system. First, Canada experienced particularly acutely the global economic decline associated with repeated bouts of stagflation. That is, the crafters of policy became painfully aware of three facts: (1) Canada's proximity to the US likely leaves its economic managers with less latitude for autonomous action than opposite numbers in any other advanced Western society; (2) the country still must develop essential elements of infrastructure before it can even contemplate a modern industrial strategy; and (3) unlike Britons and Americans, the electorate will not countenance any comprehensive efforts to roll back or even reassess the welfare state.

Second and relatedly, gridlock seized up the cabinet decision process. By 1978, PCO had successfully ascribed the impasse to turf battles between it and the Treasury Board Secretariat. These centred on difficulties with meshing advice to the cabinet on policy priorities and the allocation of resources. The solution that PCO served up, the Policy and Expenditure Management System, resulted in sweeping reforms between 1978 and 1980. These involved an entrenchment of the Priorities and Planning Committee's role as an inner cabinet, institution of the envelope approach to budgeting, devolution of most specific allocative decisions to sectoral committees, and creation of freestanding central agencies to provide independent policy assessments for the committees responsible for 'Economic' and 'Social' development.

The positive effects of all this added institutionalization have fallen short of gripping. Both John Turner and Brian Mulroney, in fact, have attempted to simplify the elaborate apparatus left to them by Trudeau. Of course, Mulroney's sweeping election victory in September 1984 assured him the type of strong majority position from which to mould cabinet operations to suit his stylistic preferences. Here the broad berth he has given his deputy prime minister, complete with a ministerial task force designed to cut government expenditure, could mean that this government will rely less on 'communities of interest' and more on central guidance in its search for fiscal discipline. If so, sectoral committees will make their decisions much less independently than under Trudeau — even if they continue to follow the rubrics of PEMS.

References

Campbell, Colin (1980) 'Political Leadership in Canada: Pierre Elliot Trudeau and the Ottawa Model', in R. Rose and E. Suleiman (eds), *Presidents and Prime Ministers*. Washington DC: American Enterprise Institute.

Campbell, Colin (1983) *Governments Under Stress: Political Executive and Key Bureaucrats in Washington, London and Ottawa*. Toronto: University of Toronto Press.

Campbell, Colin and George J. Szablowski (1979) *The Superbureaucrats: Structure and Behaviour in Central Agencies*. Toronto: Macmillan.

Chapman, Richard A. and J.R. Greenaway (1980) *The Dynamics of Administrative Reform*. London: Croom Helm.

Dawson, R. MacGregor (1963) *The Government of Canada.* Toronto: University of Toronto Press.

Dobuzinskis, Laurent (1977) 'Rational Policy-Making: Policy, Politics, and Political Science', pp. 211–28 in Thomas A. Hockin (ed.), *Apex of Power: The Prime Minister and Political Leadership in Canada.* Scarborough, Ontario: Prentice-Hall.

Doern, G. Bruce (1983) 'The Mega-Project Episode and the Formulation of Canadian Economic Development Policy', *Canadian Public Administration*, 26: 219–38.

Doern, G. Bruce (1984) 'Energy Expenditures and the NEP: Controlling the Energy Leviathan', pp. 31–78 in Allan M. Maslove (ed.), *How Ottawa Spends, 1984: The New Agenda.* Toronto: Methuen.

French, Richard D. (1979) 'The Privy Council Office: Support for Cabinet Decision Making', pp. 363–94 in Richard A. Schultz, Orest M. Kruhlak and John C. Terry (eds), *The Canadian Political Process.* Toronto: Holt, Rinehart and Winston.

Granatstein, J.L. (1981) *A Man of Influence: Norman A. Robertson and Canadian Statecraft, 1929–68.* Ottawa: Deneau.

Granatstein, J.L. (1982) *The Ottawa Men: The Civil Service Mandarins, 1935–57.* Toronto: Oxford.

Heeney, A.D.P. (1946) 'Cabinet Government in Canada: Some Developments in the Machinery of the Central Executive', *Canadian Journal of Economics and Political Science*, 12: 282–301.

Lijphart, Arend (1977) *Democracy in Plural Societies: A Comparative Exploration.* New Haven: Yale University Press.

Lithwick, N. Harvey and John Devlin (1984) 'Economic Development Policy: A Case Study in Underdeveloped Policy-making', pp. 122–66 in Allan M. Maslove (ed.), *How Ottawa Spends, 1984: The New Agenda.* Toronto: Methuen.

Mackintosh, John P. (1977) *The British Cabinet.* London: Stevens.

Mallory, J.R. (1971) *The Structure of Canadian Government.* Toronto: Macmillan.

Matheson, W.A. (1976) *The Prime Minister and the Cabinet.* Toronto: Methuen.

Morton, W.L. (1955) 'The Formation of the First Federal Cabinet', *Canadian Historical Review*, 36: 113–25.

Newman, Peter C. (1963) *Renegade in Power: The Diefenbaker Years.* Toronto: McClelland and Stewart.

Pitfield, Michael (1976) 'The Shape of Government in the 1980's: Techniques and Instruments for Policy Formation at the Federal Level', *Canadian Public Administration*, 19: 8–20.

Prince, Michael, J. (1984) 'Whatever Happened to Compassion? Liberal Social Policy, 1980–4', pp. 79–121 in Allan M. Maslove (ed.), *How Ottawa Spends, 1984: The New Agenda.* Toronto: Methuen.

Punnett, R.M. (1977) *The Prime Minister in Canadian Government and Politics.* Toronto: Macmillan.

Robertson, R.G. (1971) 'The Changing Role of the Privy Council', *Canadian Public Administration*, 14: 487–508.

Szablowski, George J. (1977) 'The Optimal Policy-Making System: Implications for the Canadian Political Process', pp. 197–211 in Thomas A. Hockin (ed.), *Apex of Power: The Prime Minister and Political Leadership in Canada.* Scarborough, Ontario: Prentice-Hall.

Turner, John (1980) *Lloyd George's Secretariat*. Cambridge: Cambridge University Press.

Van Loon, Richard (1981) 'Stop the Music: The Current Policy and Expenditure Management System in Ottawa', *Canadian Public Administration*, 24: 175–99.

Wilson, V. Seymour (1981) *Canadian Public Policy and Administration: Theory and Environment*. Toronto: McGraw-Hill Ryerson.

6
Cabinet committees in Australia and New Zealand

Patrick Weller

6.1 Introduction

Australia and New Zealand share a common cabinet heritage; both have derived their practices and principles from the British model. They accept the doctrines of collective and ministerial responsibility and the belief that cabinet ought to be the final and authoritative decision-making body. The cabinets are chaired by the prime ministers, supported by a cabinet secretariat and accepted as the apex of power. But thereafter there are substantial differences.

Both countries have much smaller populations than Britain and this fact has an important impact on their political systems; New Zealand has a Parliament of ninety-two members (ninety-five after 1984) and a cabinet of up to twenty ministers and two under secretaries. The government party may have as few as forty-seven people from which to draw its cabinet. In Australia the two houses contain around 190 members (increased by thirty-seven in 1984); the ministry has twenty-seven people in it, of whom thirteen or fourteen are in the cabinet. But in Australia the greatest difference of all is that the Parliament and ministry must work within the limiting provisions of a federal system enshrined in a written constitution over which not they, but the courts, have final powers of interpretation.

Cabinet serves a variety of additional roles. It acts as the chief arbiter of disputes and as the final source of authority. It is a clearing-house for decisions effectively taken elsewhere, but which need cabinet endorsement or noting. It acts as an information exchange, so that ministers may become aware of what the executive as a whole is thinkng and doing. It may serve (to use a New Zealand expression) as a comfort stop. In small systems, the choice of ministers may be limited. In Australia they often have to fulfil a representative function (Weller and Grattan, 1981: 26–28); in New Zealand the lack of a field may mean the prime minister has no real choice at all (Jackson, 1978: 66). Weaker ministers may bring submissions to cabinet, preferring the security of collective support to the uncertainty and potential pitfalls of individual decision.

Cabinets in Australia and New Zealand therefore probably make more collective decisions and certainly consider many more items than their counterparts in Britain and Canada. They have a solidifying and supportive role. To understand where cabinet committees fit into the framework in each country, it is therefore necessary to understand the environment in which cabinet works, particularly their functions and workload. After all, if the intended purpose of cabinet is to reduce the pressure on the full cabinet, we need to ask what that entails.

6.2 **Australia**

6.2.1 *Context and workload*

In Australia cabinet meets often and considers a wide range of items. The Cabinet Handbook prescribes those items that need to be considered by cabinet or its committees. These are:

(a) new policy proposals and proposed significant variations to existing policies;

(b) proposals likely to have a significant effect on employment in either the public or private sector;

(c) expenditure proposals, including proposals for major capital works and computer acquisitions (normally considered only in the budget context, that is, when draft estimates of ongoing policies and programmes and new policy proposals are being considered);

(d) proposals requiring legislation, other than minor proposals which the prime minister has agreed need not be raised in cabinet (procedures to be followed in handling such proposals are set out in the *Legislation Handbook*);

(e) proposals likely to have a considerable impact upon relations between the Commonwealth and foreign, State or local governments; and

(f) proposed responses to recommendations made in parliamentary committee reports, except for responses which the prime minister agrees raise no significant policy questions (Cabinet Handbook, 1983: 9).

In earlier governments these guidelines were marginally different. Under the Fraser governments expenditure proposals that did not exceed $1,500,000 for the next three years could be introduced with the approval of the minister for finance (Cabinet Handbook, 1982: 150). That concession was one effort to reduce the cabinet workload. But the general categories have remained the same (see also Hawker, Smith and Weller, 1979; Fraser, 1978).

However, even if these were the only items that ministers *had* to bring to cabinet, it did not follow that they were the only submissions they brought. Ministers could and did bring a wide range of other issues to cabinet for consideration because they wanted its support. As one leading minister commented:

> I find it hard to believe that the good government of a country needs as many cabinet or cabinet committee decisions as it gets. But, on the other hand, as matters do come before cabinet it is one way of making sure that all ministers understand what is happening and what it is about. It gives the minister the reassurance of his cabinet colleagues and it is important therefore for the cabinet system and for cabinet solidarity if ministers have been part of a decision (quoted in Weller and Grattan, 1981: 136).

Partly as a result, cabinet meetings are frequent; Table 6.1 lists the number of meetings held by the Whitlam, Fraser and Hawke cabinets and cabinet committees between 1973 and July 1983. Generally there were almost two cabinet meetings each week and between four and seven meetings of various cabinet committees. The frequency of meetings was particularly high under the Fraser government and in 1979 a review of cabinet procedures was undertaken by the secretary of the Department of Prime Minister and Cabinet. For a time the number of meetings declined, but it rose again in 1981–2.

The ministers also have to read for a wide range of submissions. The chore is often regarded as excessive, and some ministers readily admit that they do not read and understand every item that cabinet is to discuss (Weller and Grattan, 1981: 110). Tables 6.2 and 6.3 indicate why they have a problem. Of course, lists of submissions and papers may provide a misleading impression; some are important, others are not. But they provide an indication of how busy cabinet is and how many decisions, of one type or another, are made.

Some of the decisions may be routine: to receive a report, to note information or to determine a time for meeting. Others may have been thrashed out in committee and only need endorsement. But many decisions are not as simple to reach. They deal with items of political sensitivity or are needed to bolster a weaker minister. It is amidst this picture of a very busy cabinet that the development and processes of committees need to be considered.

6.2.2 Development and processes

In Australia the size of cabinet and the extent of business did not require a sophisticated support system before 1939; but the rapid

TABLE 6.1
Meetings of cabinet and cabinet committees

Time	Weeks	Full Ministry	Cabinet	Standing Committee	Ad Hoc	Total
Whitlam Government						
Dec. 1972–Apr. 1974	70	N/A	69	130	23	222
May 1974–Sept. 1975	73	N/A	59	58	82	199
Total	143		128	188	105	421
Fraser Government						
Dec. 1975–Nov. 1976	48	8	57	68	21	154
Nov. 1976–Oct. 1977	48	9	112	100	56	277
Oct. 1977–Dec. 1978	64	11	164	174	132	481
1979	52	15	97	324		436
1980	52	11	70	246		327
1981	52	10	112	310		428
Jan. 1982–Mar. 1983	61	6	111	218		335
Hawke Government						
March–June 1983	16	6	19	99		124

Source: See note 1.

TABLE 6.2
Submissions to cabinet

Time	Weeks	Submissions	Papers		Av. per week
McMahon Government					
Oct. 1971–Oct. 1972	52	550	—		11
Whitlam Government					
Dec. 1972–2 Oct. 1974	86	1304	—		15
June 1974–May 1975	52	662	—		13
May 1975–Sept. 1975	13	284	—		22
Fraser Government				Total	
Dec. 1975–Dec. 1976	54	972	28	1000	19
1977	52	877	194	1071	21
1978	52	1045	618	1663	32
1979	52	709	678	1377	27
1980	52	735	638	1373	26
1981	52	762	957	1719	33
1982–March 1983	61	741	680	1421	23
Hawke Government					
March–June 1983	16	263	149	422	26

Source: See note 1.

TABLE 6.3
Number of cabinet decisions

Time	Weeks	With Submission or Paper	Without Submission Appts	Other	Total	Average per week
McMahon Government						
Oct. 1971–Oct. 1972	52	—	—	—	983	19
Whitlam Government						
Dec. 1972–Apr. 1974	70	835	137	328	1300	19
May 1974–Sept. 1975	73	789	158	188	1135	16
Total	143	1624	295	516	2435	
Fraser Government						
Dec. 1975–Nov. 1976	48	767	307		1074	22
Nov. 1976– Oct. 1977	48	1011	711		1722	36
Oct. 1977–Dec.1978	64	1304	589		1893	30
1979	52	1809(+108)*	196	924	3037	59
1980	52	1358(+219)*	194	674	2445	47
1981	52	2497(+205)*	224	930	3839#	74
Jan. 1982–Mar. 1983	61	1254(+251)*	222	695	2398	39
Hawke Government						
March-June 1983	16	489(+50)*	77	177	793	50

Notes: * Legislation committee decisions.
\# Of these decisions, 1007 decisions were made by the Committee on the Review of
Commonwealth Functions or by cabinet on RCF related matters.
Source: See note 1.

growth of the scope of federal government during the war led to the
development of more elaborate arrangements. In the war there
were two main cabinet committees: the war cabinet and the
production executive. Both had considerable authority and the right
to make final decisions. At the same time the first cabinet
secretariat was established to provide support; before then the
prime minister had taken note of the decisions himself.

In the post-war Chifley government (1945–9) the full ministry of
nineteen sat in cabinet. Chifley's arrangements included a set of
committees which had evolved from the wartime system. These
were the Defence Council and four economic committees — Trade
and Employment, Industry and Employment, Secondary Indus-
tries, and Dollar Budget. Other ad hoc committees were appointed
from time to time. Although it is not clear to what extent
committees took final decisions, it seems that some of them did.
(The following sections are based on Hawker, Smith and Weller,
1979: 59–86.)

Full cabinet as a collectivity received little bureaucratic support. The secretary to cabinet saw his responsibility as the collection and circulation of submissions and the recording of decisions. He believed that the support of cabinet committees should be the function of the department of the minister chairing the committee and did not try to build up a major coordinating role for the Department of Prime Minister and Cabinet (PMC) (Crisp, 1967: 31–2). As a result, cabinet committees were served in more depth than was full cabinet.

The working of the cabinet committee system depended as much on the way ministers and officials approached their tasks as on formal structures. The committees' secretarial services were provided by the department of the convening minister (for the economic committees, usually Treasury or Post-War Reconstruction). More importantly, committees were supported by parallel committees of senior officials and, below them, by groups of 'offsiders', often the protegés of senior officials. At many committee meetings ministers were accompanied not only by senior officials but by 'offsiders' as well, and some of these meetings took on the character of 'mass seminars' (Crisp, 1967: 49). The whole group has been described as Chifley's 'official family'.

The Chifley cabinet's procedures succeeded for four reasons: Chifley's leadership; a pool of talented and probing public servants; a common set of activist ideas, especially about economic management; and the broadening scope of government activity, a legacy of wartime events. Although the failure of some of Chifley's policies and the 1949 defeat warn against exaggerating the success of such a system, the combination of these factors meant that cabinet, more than its predecessors, had the capacity to draw together the various threads of policy.

When Menzies came to power in 1949, he was unenthusiastic about officials attending any formally constituted ministerial meetings, and although the network of officials established under Labor did not immediately disappear, the distinctive mixing of formal and informal relationships of the Chifley period soon vanished. Moreover, although Menzies set up initially no less than nineteen cabinet committees, this profuse growth soon withered. The taking of important decisions shifted back to full cabinet (Crisp, 1967).

Two other steps in the evolution of cabinet were taken. First, Menzies divided his ministers into an inner cabinet and an outer ministry in 1955, when the size of the ministry had risen to twenty-two. Cabinet itself was reduced to twelve and remained at that number even when the rest of the ministry increased. Non-cabinet ministers attended cabinet meetings only by invitation, usually to participate in discussion of items of business concerning their departments. The system tried to balance the advantages of a small, powerful cabinet against the disadvantages of non-cabinet ministers not fully appreciating the context in which discussion on their items took place and thus proceeding with departmental work in isolation. Menzies's personal ascendancy in the government ensured that the system worked well enough for him.

The introduction of the system reduced the importance of cabinet committees. Menzies continued to operate both standing and ad hoc committees, but, as Crisp has pointed out, the list was 'rather thin, thin more especially in the economic policy and coordination field where the Chifley picture was strong'. Crisp has listed five committees known to exist in the mid-1960s: Defence and Foreign Affairs; Legislation; General Administrative; Economic Policy; and Ex-Servicemen's. Of these the General Administrative Committee was the most interesting. Crisp has described it as 'a large busy committee made up of some cabinet and most or all non-Cabinet Ministers. It [met] weekly during Parliamentary Sessions to despatch very usefully a great deal of "second order" business' (Crisp, 1967: 49). Its task was to relieve cabinet of business that required the authority of a cabinet decision but did not have a substantial policy content or need sustained attention.

Second, Menzies enhanced cabinet's capacity by widening the context in which cabinet considered the annual budget. Whereas Chifley had made one main submission on the budget, under Menzies the number and range of submissions increased dramatically, including the introduction of a statement of total cash prospects for the federal government. This presented a wider analysis than the statement of consolidated revenue which hitherto had been cabinet's main starting point. Cabinet also regularly received papers on the state of the economy and reviewed economic prospects before making actual budget allocations. Managing the economy became recognized as a year-round occupation. The fullness of cabinet's consideration of the budget contrasted with the much smaller role given to British cabinets (see 4.4.3) and was regarded with great satisfaction by senior Treasury officers (see R.J. Randall, quoted in Crisp, 1961: 325).

After Menzies' retirement in 1966 his successors, Holt (1966–7), Gorton (1968–71) and McMahon (1971–2), made few attempts to alter the cabinet structure. Little is known about the existence of cabinet committees, although one minister later complained that McMahon tried to delegate to committees but, if he did not like the answer, kept reopening the items in cabinet (Weller and Grattan, 1981: 126). With cabinet going over those decisions made in committee, and with the government anyway factionalized and inert, few decisions were made and the usefulness of a committee system disappeared.

Under Whitlam considerable thought was given to the creation of a cabinet committee system. The importance of a system of committees for a large and busy cabinet had been recognized by Whitlam before he took office. From the outset, Labor used cabinet committees more extensively and more openly than the coalition government. But the experience showed the ease with which apparently admirable arrangements could fall into disuse. Matching up procedural and political incentives in support of a workable committee system proved more difficult than was first thought. Ministers had not only to be convinced of the usefulness and fairness of a committee system but also had to find time for committee meetings in schedules of work that were already overcrowded. The longer parliamentary sitting times introduced by Labor combined with meetings of full cabinet, caucus, and caucus committees presented ministers with punishing rounds of meetings each week.

The Whitlam cabinet began work with a system of five standing committees — Economic, Welfare, Urban and Regional Development, Foreign Affairs and Defence, and Legislation. The intention was to establish a framework 'which [would] facilitate logical ministerial consideration (if ministers wish[ed] to exercise their powers) of all major recommendations, alternatives to them, and their side-effects on other policy areas' (*Canberra Times*, 12 January 1973). The committees were explicitly based on federal Canadian experience. It was proposed to establish standing committees in all policy areas, to route all cabinet business through committees, to ensure participation in decision-making by all ministers through regular meetings and to create, where appropriate, coordinating committees. At a press conference the prime minister described the proposed system in the following terms:

> The procedure will be that when submissions for cabinet come to me from ministers I will send them to the relevant committee. The committee will hopefully make a recommendation on them. They will then be listed on the cabinet agenda and the recommendation also listed, and unless anybody wants it debated further the recommendation will become the cabinet decision.... The members of the committee are under an obligation to attend the meetings of the committee but any other minister will be entitled to attend and hopefully will do so when the documents indicate his department is involved. (*Canberra Times*, 12 January 1973).

The intention was to avoid overcrowding cabinet's agenda without

TABLE 6.4
Committee decisions altered or confirmed by cabinet

Decisions	Confirmed		Altered			
	Oral Report	Written Report	Oral Report	Written Report	Total	Per cent altered
Dec. 1972–Apr. 1974	91	279	10	77	457	19.0
May 1974–Sept. 1975	11	63	4	20	98	24.5

Source: See note 1.

excluding any minister with a valid interest in business before a particular committee. It was accepted that problems might include competing demands on ministerial time, the possibilities of a slowing down of decision-making and of excessive public service influence on committee deliberations, and the risk of obvious divergences of view between ministers and their senior public servants. As the originator of the proposal, Peter Wilenski (later Whitlam's principal private secretary), commented:

> Whether the system works is finally up to ministers. It is unlikely (after the first month or two) that all ministers will wish to attend all meetings, which would clog up the system. The greater danger is that they may give the committees a decreasing amount of attention — but of course any cabinet has the right to decide what control it wishes to have over policy and what aspects they wish to pass to the Public Service. (*Canberra Times*, 12 January 1973).

During 1973 the arrangements worked reasonably well; however, after the election in May 1974 the system withered. From mid-1974 ad hoc committees became much more important than they had previously been. This is illustrated succinctly by comparing the work of ad hoc committees before and after June 1974. In the period before June 1974 they met forty-seven times and made twenty-nine decisions; in the period from June 1974 to May 1975 they met sixty-two times and made 117 decisions. From mid-1974 only the legislation committee among the standing committees continued to have an active and effective life. As with similar committees under the Liberals, its functions were mainly technical and procedural. Although the decline of the other standing committees was decisive it was never the subject of cabinet discussion and none of the committees was ever formally disbanded.

Even though committees did not have the authority to make final decisions, their recommendations were usually accepted. Table 6.4 shows both the 'success' rate of their proposals and the marked decline in their use. The system of standing committees failed for several reasons. It depended entirely on the prime minister's willingness to refer items to them; but he chose not to utilize the system. Its meetings were never properly integrated into the parliamentary schedule, and often met just before full cabinet; as a result there were no clear recommendations circulated in advance. Besides, as committees could not make final decisions, their existence did not reduce cabinet's workload and ministers saw little point in attending them. The reasons were both procedural and political.

As a consequence Whitlam relied instead on ad hoc committees and informal gatherings of ministers of his own choosing. In 1975 three ad hoc committees, with a continuing existence and with parallel committees of officials in support, became particularly influential. These were the Expenditure Review Committee (ERC), the Australian State Regional Relations Committee and the Resources Committee. Their existence, unlike the most normal temporary ad hoc committees, was publicly announced (for greater detail, see Hawker *et al.*, 1979: 83–87).

The ERC was the most important. Its members included the prime minister, the treasurer, and the ministers for social security, labour and immigration, and urban and regional development. Set up by cabinet in January 1975 when the government had decided that its earlier open-handed approach to public expenditure could no longer be maintained, the committee was to examine all proposals for expenditure both during and outside the budget round. It was intended to keep strict limits on government spending. The working of the committee conferred considerable influence on a small number of selected ministers. If it rejected a proposal for expenditure, the prime minister tended not to list the item for full cabinet unless the minister concerned persisted. In a time of expenditure restraint, ministerial persistence was not common. Committee decisions effectively became cabinet decisions. The creation of the ERC was a limited but definite step towards the creation of a group that could give detailed attention to priorities. The concentration of power in the hands of a ministerial élite was accepted in the atmosphere of crisis that prevailed in 1975, but might have become divisive in the longer term. It did, however, provide a model for committees of later governments.

Fraser (Prime Minister from 1975 to 1983) went into office publicly committed to the concept of collective cabinet government. He had written that 'how' things were done was important. He reinstated the inner cabinet and insisted from the beginning that ministers adhere to a rigid code of discipline.

When first elected, Fraser announced the formation of six cabinet committees; he himself was to act as chairman of the four most important — those on planning and coordination, economics, foreign affairs and defence, and machinery of government. The other two, the general administrative committee and the legislation committee, were chaired by senior colleagues. The choice of members of these committees indicated how far the members of cabinet who were less sympathetic to the prime minister were isolated from the process of decision.

After the 1977 election Fraser changed the structure. Committees on planning and coordination, foreign affairs and defence, and machinery of government were retained; a new committee concerned with intelligence and security was also created. Fraser was chairman of all these four. But the economic committee of cabinet was abolished; as Fraser pointed out, it had 'touched on so many portfolios that it became akin to cabinet itself. For that reason cabinet as a whole normally deals with economic issues' (Fraser, 1978: 10). In its place two smaller committees to deal with economic affairs were appointed — a monetary committee responsible for interest, bank and currency exchange rates (with Fraser as chairman) and a wages committee for industrial and wages policy (chaired by the deputy leader of the Liberal Party). Other committees dealt with government purchasing, social welfare (both newly created), general administrative matters and legislation.

After the 1980 election a further set of changes were made; the new structure included the Coordination committee, the Foreign Affairs and Defence committee (now including intelligence and security), Monetary Policy, Legislation, Welfare Policy, Industry Policy, and General Policy. Fraser was chairman of the first three. Of these, the most important was the Coordination committee; it formalized the earlier situation in which the party leaders had met to discuss longer term aims and gave those deliberations authority. Each committee's terms of reference were made public.

For much of Fraser's period as prime minister the standing committees were shadowed by permanent heads committees. All but one of those shadowing committees was chaired by the secretary of the Department of Prime Minister and Cabinet. However the officials committees never became so formalized that they acted as an inevitable channel to the relevant committees, screening and discussing material before it reached the ministers. Submissions to cabinet were required to include details of which ministers and departments had been consulted and reference to the views of other bodies where disagreements occurred; this demand was considered an adequate means of ensuring that ministers would be aware of differences of opinion and that consultations would take place.

The Cabinet Handbook of 1982 stated that 'as a general rule, standing committees take final decisions on matters referred to them. Committees from time to time will, however, judge that a matter, because of its policy significance, should not be finally determined in committee but should be referred for full Cabinet consideration' (1982: 159). In all circumstances committees were regarded as the same as the full cabinet in terms of authority. It was not the practice 'to indicate whether a matter was taken in a committee rather than Cabinet' (1982: 156).

In the Fraser government, cabinet submissions were allocated to full cabinet or its committees according to their subject matter and political importance. Where committees had the right to make final decisions, that step was important. The prime minister made the decision, on the recommendation of his department; he usually accepted this recommendation. Some items were considered first by cabinet and then directed to a committee for more detailed consideration and, sometimes, for final decision. On other occasions a committee felt that an item needed full cabinet approval. The decisions of cabinet committees were recorded on white paper, an indication of their status as final. All ministers received copies of all committee decisions, except those limited for security reasons. The decisions could be raised and discussed again in cabinet only with the approval of the prime minister. When that did occur, it was usually as an under-the-line item; that is, a question raised orally at the beginning of the agenda. When a committee decision was challenged, it was usually deferred for further review by the committee, rather than changed. That did not happen often.

The standing committees were usually supplemented by the creation of ad hoc committees. They served a variety of functions: to finalize details of an issue which had been decided in principle, to work through complicated items so that the main issues could be identified for later cabinet decision or for expenditure review. In 1980, for instance, the main ad hoc committees were concerned with the New Parliament House, with Taxation (to consider matters of taxation policy and legislation, particularly in relation to tax avoidance issues), and the Budget committee (to review expenditure) (Cabinet Handbook, 1982: 162–3). Each year an ad hoc committee was appointed to review the forward estimates in a pre-budget attempt to reduce expenditure. In 1981 a Review of Commonwealth Functions was intended to examine the whole range of government activities and to recommend changes. The review was very public and its report was tabled in Parliament.

Ad hoc committees tended to be disbanded once their task had been fulfilled. It is therefore difficult to be precise about the number that were in existence at any time; one suggestion was that there were usually less than a dozen formally constituted, of which only half a dozen were likely to be active. Ad hoc committees normally did not have the power to make final decisions, unless it was specified in their terms of reference. The exceptions tended to be the Expenditure Review committees which were granted authority to make decisions. But even then ministers could ensure that, when they disagreed with the decision, their preferences were brought to budget cabinet as a disagreed bid,[2] so that they could in effect try to overturn the committees' decision.

Comparative figures for decisions of standing and ad hoc committees are rare. What is available, in Table 6.5, suggests that in the Fraser government's first three years, the workload of the standing committees increased gradually, but there was a sudden increase in ad hoc activity in 1978, perhaps due to the expenditure review that followed the 1977 election. A similar increase, noted in Table 6.3, followed the decisions of the Review of Commonwealth Functions. The two types of committee therefore operated effectively side by side.

TABLE 6.5
Committee decisions under Fraser government

Period	Weeks	Ad Hoc With submission	Ad Hoc Without submission	Standing With submission	Standing Without submission	Legislation committee	Total
Dec. 1975–Nov. 1976	48	35	41	260	99	254	689
Nov. 1976–Oct. 1977	48	83	66	280	65	197	691
Oct. 1977–Dec. 1978	64	341	143	313	179	316	1292

Source: See note 1.

Before the election of the Hawke Labor government in 1983 a task force on government administration was established to plan the details of the possible transition, including a proposed set of cabinet committees: it assumed that the Labor government would have all its twenty-seven ministers in cabinet (as the Whitlam government had done), but by the time of the election victory an inner cabinet had been adopted (Weller, 1983: 309–10). The task force proposed a Priorities and Planning committee, but the need for it was removed by the assumption that the smaller cabinet would satisfy the requirement for central direction. Three coordinating committees were created: Expenditure Review, Parliamentary Business, and Legislation; and six functional committees: Economic Policy, Industry Policy, Infrastructure Policy, Social Policy, Legal and Administrative, and Defence and Foreign Affairs. The latter included an Intelligence and Security sub-committee, which later was given independent status.

The prime minister was nominally chairman of all but one of the committees, the exception being the Legislation committee which was chaired by the Attorney-General. Each committee has clear responsibilities that have been publicly announced and regular meeting times. The Parliamentary Business committee meets each Monday of a sitting week to plan the tactical decisions required to get the governments programme through Parliament. The Expenditure committee played an important role in the budget process, reviewing programmes and meeting ministers to discuss possible cuts.

The Cabinet Handbook (1983: 2) explains how the process should work:

1.7 Each Submission from a Minister is allocated by the Prime Minister to one of the functional or co-ordinating committees for consideration. Matters are referred to particular functional committees on the basis of their essential character rather than simply by reference to departments from which they originate. Subject to the reservations referred to in paragraph 1.11 below, decisions of functional committees and some co-ordinating committees are subsequently put to Cabinet for endorsement. As far as possible, issues are resolved at the committee stage and not taken to Cabinet until the committee has reached its decision on all aspects.

1.8 Functional committee decisions involving expenditure of more than $100,000 in any financial year additional to expenditure announced in the Budget, and decisions involving increased costs to the Budget on the revenue side, are considered by the Expenditure Review Committee before being put to Cabinet for endorsement.

1.9 The committee system is designed to ensure that decisions are reached after thorough discussion and on the basis of general consensus. Cabinet endorsement of committee decisions is then normally a formal process not involving the re-opening of discussion. If there are aspects of a committee decision which a Minister wishes to raise in Cabinet, the Minister informs the Prime Minister or the Secretary to Cabinet in writing beforehand. The matter may then be formally raised when the decision is put for endorsement. If the request is made by a non-Cabinet Minister, that Minister is co-opted as a matter of course to attend the Cabinet meeting for that item.

1.10 Changes of substance are not normally made in endorsing a committee decision unless the Minister responsible for the original proposal is present. If a matter of substance is at issue, Cabinet normally refers the matter back to the committee for further consideration.

Similarly, if there is a Cabinet request for an additional Submission or Memorandum, or for an Addendum to a document already before it, the matter, in the normal course, is returned to the appropriate functional committee for consideration before being considered by Cabinet again.

1.11 Decisions of the Legislation Committee need not be further considered in Cabinet, the policy issues involved having already been endorsed there. Some decisions of the Parliamentary Business Committee, decisions of the National and International Security Committee relating to sensitive matters, and some special decisions of other committees (for example, exchange rate decisions of the Economic Policy Committee), are not submitted for Cabinet endorsement. The committees themselves may decide, however, that a particular decision within their authority should be referred to Cabinet for endorsement.

Generally the committees were to meet on weekdays and their recommendations, recorded on blue paper to indicate their provisional nature, were then to be taken to the next Monday meeting of cabinet for endorsement. The prime minister reads through each agenda item to provide an opportunity for debate but usually none occurs.

The rules laid down by the Handbook have largely been followed in the first year of the Hawke government. Almost all items are directed to the relevant committee by the prime minister, on the recommendation of his department. Very occasionally items have been taken direct to cabinet, but that can only be done with the approval of the prime minister. Committees usually manage to reach a decision and few items are referred to cabinet. If twenty or thirty decisions are brought to cabinet for endorsement, it is unlikely that more than two or three will be re-raised in cabinet; sometimes none are. Since ministers were involved in the creation of the system, several of them are also committed to making it work. Attempts to bypass established procedures, though rare, are opposed by cabinet colleagues as well as by the prime minister.

The prime minister still chairs most of the meetings of committees. Since many of the important issues are now discussed there, that involvement is regarded as essential. Further his undoubted skills as a chairman have assisted in the comparatively smooth working of the system. Since he likes business to be predictable, he ensures his ministers benefit from predictable procedures too.

The delegation of the majority of decisions to committees has not been without some problems. Since committees are not able to take final decisions, it is the first time in Australia that some ministers outside cabinet in effect do not participate in taking any cabinet decisions. Even when access to cabinet has gradually relaxed (see Weller, 1981 for discussion), there has been some discontent among non-cabinet ministers about their lack of involvement. Meetings of the whole ministry are therefore more common than under Fraser and in January 1984, following the Canadian precedent, the whole ministry held a political strategy meeting without officials and private staff. At that meeting a committee of ministers was created to consider how the outer ministers could better become integrated into the cabinet decision-making system.

Ad hoc committees have been rare in the Hawke government, an indication that the standing committees appear capable of dealing with the government business. One ad hoc, on industrial restructuring, has the capacity to examine the problem more widely than any of the standing committees; its function is to bring a report to cabinet. Its existence is exceptional.

6.2.3 *Membership*

There is little available information about the membership of the cabinet committees before 1972; thereafter the names of the ministers of all the standing committees have been announced when a new government took office.

In the Whitlam government there is no indication that any ministers were deliberately excluded from a standing committee to which they had a functional claim as a result of the portfolio they held. Some ministers were on committees in different capacities; the deputy prime minister was on two committees in that role and one other as minister of defence. Where the prime minister had had an influence was in the initial allocation of portfolios.

The same was not true of the ad hoc committees; the selection of their membership gave greater scope to the prime minister. The attendance at ad hoc committees was limited to the official membership. Therefore the selection of ministers to bodies like the Expenditure Review committee was significant as an indication of the prime minister's trust and of the weight that ministers wielded at the time. There were few complaints at the time, but if access to such an essential committee had remained limited, complaints would probably have occurred. At the same time the prime minister occasionally created kitchen cabinet committees in which the membership floated. Such meetings had no formal status in the committee system, but did at times pre-digest important issues.

In the Fraser cabinet too, most standing committees were determined on functional grounds, or could be justified primarily on those grounds. Some committees were clearly regarded as more junior; the Welfare committee only included three cabinet ministers among its fourteen members in 1984, and the General Policy committee only four out of fourteen. But they did allow some non-cabinet members greater participation in collective decision-making at a lower level, even though their portfolios had little direct relation to the subject matters.

Other committees were more prestigious. In Foreign Affairs and Defence in 1980, eleven of the twelve were cabinet members. The former minister for foreign affairs, Andrew Peacock (who had moved to be minister for industrial relations), was not on it but the minister for primary industry, Peter Nixon, was. He was a close colleague of the prime minister. Peacock also complained in his resignation speech in 1981 that he had been deliberately excluded from the Monetary committee (*Commonwealth Parliamentary Debates*, 28 April 1981: 1608) and, despite promises that he would be added, never was. However Nixon again was. His inclusion was presumably both personal and a means of retaining a coalition balance on the committees. It seems therefore that, although few were left out, others could be added to the important committees.

Of all the committees the Coordination committee was seen as the most central. Peacock claimed, again when he resigned, that at times the prime minister had asked cabinet ministers to leave the room so that the Coordination committee could discuss sensitive items. The prime minister and his colleagues denied it. But membership was exclusive; it consisted of the prime minister, the deputy prime minister (who was leader of the National Party), the deputy leaders of the Liberal and National parties, and the government leader in the Senate. Other ministers attended at various occasions. It discussed much parliamentary business and many under-the-line (i.e. without submission) items.

In the Hawke government the membership of the standing committees were almost all determined by the portfolios that ministers held. Some ministers were therefore only on one committee and others were on three. The main exception was the minister of finance who was on every committee except the Defence and Foreign Affairs committee. The only choice that did not have a portfolio basis was the inclusion of the former party leader and treasurer, Bill Hayden, on the Economic committee; that was justified on the grounds of tact and political common sense.

6.3 New Zealand[3]

6.3.1 *Environment*

In New Zealand the pace of cabinet is often as hectic as in Australia. At its regular weekly meetings cabinet usually considers some thirty-five items which require a formal minute. Of these about 75 per cent go through without significant change. Towards the end of a parliamentary session, when there is some pressure to settle finally a range of proposals, the agenda tends to increase. Towards the end

TABLE 6.6
Cabinet workload in New Zealand

Cabinet submissions listed in cabinet agenda	1357
Bills listed in cabinet agenda	83
Total	1440
Regular cabinet meetings held	48
Average per meeting	30
Cabinet minutes issued	1688
plus supplementary memoranda	141
Total formal decisions	1829
Average per meeting	38

(There were also three other special cabinet meetings with one submission and minute each)

Cabinet committee submissions	1106
plus bills listed in CCLPQ agenda	117
Total	1223
Cabinet committee meetings held	262
Average over 48 working weeks	5

Source: New Zealand Cabinet Offices.

of a calendar year it can take on the appearance of a clearance sale with up to ninety items to be considered at the final meeting.

The figures for one year can give some indication of the workload. In 1979, not an election year, the cabinet workload was as in Table 6.6. Not all of these items are of great importance; they may include subjects 'such as Ministerial overseas travel, appointments to Quangos, Ministerial representation at functions, as well as draft regulations' (Galvin, 1982: 13). Their appearance on the agenda illustrates an important aspect of New Zealand politics: the desire for collective involvement as a means of creating a feeling of security for ministers. In part this requirement is created by the comparative lack of talent in the New Zealand Parliament. An incoming prime minister may have to choose, or a Labor caucus elect, a cabinet of twenty, two under secretaries, the speaker, two whips and a chairman of committees from a field of less than thirty experienced MPs (Jackson, 1978), effectively no choice at all. As a result many of the ministers are weak and require the consistent support of their colleagues. The New Zealand cabinet therefore seems to be more often involved in the making of decisions and to retain a greater sense of cohesion than many of its counterparts elsewhere. They all work in the same building, the Beehive; they often eat together, and as a result have a greater opportunity to interact with one another than in many similar systems.

6.3.2 *Development and processes*

In New Zealand there are traditionally five reasons for the establishment of cabinet committees: to relieve the cabinet agenda; to enable key ministers to become acquainted with complex issues before they come to cabinet; to enable groups of ministers and officials to discuss issues which cut across portfolios; to give newer ministers broader and deeper experience of the executive; and political convenience. The logic is therefore both traditional and helps ensure solidarity; the committees act both as a means of getting decisions made and encouraging greater cohesion in the cabinet (Galvin, 1982: 21).

In New Zealand the cabinet committee system dates from 1950. When Sidney Holland became prime minister, he initially appointed sixteen standing committees. By 1954 the number had increased to eighteen standing and nearly twice as many ad hoc committees. The premier committee has usually been the Cabinet Economic committee (CEC). Among the others the most influential has been the Public Works committee, which has always enjoyed a considerable degree of delegated authority. Over the next fifteen years the number of committees varied; as one minister put it, 'if you want a rapid guide to the rise and fall of contentious issues I recommend reference to the births and deaths column of Cabinet committee' (Talboys, 1970: 6).

When Sir Keith Holyoake resigned as prime minister, his cabinet had thirty-six committees in existence, largely because the distinction between standing and ad hoc committees had been dropped. One minister was even a member of twenty-three committees. In 1970 Talboys (1970: 6) recalls that twenty-three ad hoc committees had completed their work in the two years since the previous cabinet lists had been issued. Obviously committees were created for convenience and often nominally stayed in existence. But since then Talboy's comment would be less apposite because the system has stabilized.

When John Marshall became prime minister in 1972 he rationalized the system and reduced the number of committees to eleven. The Labour government elected in 1972 first created ten committees and then reduced it further to nine. But Labour did introduce one major change; the Prime Minister, Norman Kirk, established the Cabinet Committee on Policy and Priorities (CCPP). The committee had two objectives:

to establish priorities for the implementation of government policies; to keep under review the progress being made in implementing the policy programme.

The reason for creating the committee is not certain. It was proposed by Bill Rowling, the minister of finance, as a means of educating Kirk in economics. It certainly drew together the most intellectually able members of the government. It has also been suggested that its purpose was to keep out of the main 'inner' group one minister, Mick Connelly, whose portfolio and seniority required him to be a member of CEC, previously regarded as the premier committee (Roberts and Aitken, 1980: 9). A participant argued that it depended on an individual's political strength. Indeed, with that one exception, the membership of the CCPP was initially identical to that of the CEC.

At its first meeting in early 1973 it had two items on its agenda: the legislative programme and consideration of the new ministers' priorities, which had been sought soon after the party's election. The latter exercise fizzled within three months and became the 1973 expenditure review. CCPP never, according to some members, achieved the capacity to determine priorities; it should, they said, have played a strategic role, but did not have enough time. It was still learning when the oil shock of 1973 turned it into a fire brigade. Nevertheless current Labour leaders believe that a government needs some mechanism for setting priorities and suggested that a small Priorities committee should be introduced (see note 3).

Seen in perspective the CCPP was a significant but experimental phase in the development of the expenditure reviews (which have their origin in the New Zealand economic recession of 1968). These reviews took their present shape in 1972 when Marshall was prime minister and have been refined in the more difficult economic situation prevailing since 1973. Much of what the CCPP did in 1972–5 is now done by the Cabinet Committee on Expenditure and of course by CEC before and since.

When National returned to power in 1975, Robert Muldoon abolished the CCPP and returned the CEC to its former position as the premier committee of cabinet. Although there were some changes, the National cabinet adopted a structure of around thirteen standing committees. They were: Civil Defence; Communications; Defence; Economic; Expenditure; Family and Social Affairs; Honours; Legislation and Parliamentary Questions; Science and Technology; State Services; Terrorism; Transport; and Works. Each committee had between four (Honours) and ten (Civil Defence, Works) members. In addition there were a few ad hoc committees set up for particular and limited purposes: for instance, at one stage there was a committee to react to the Danks Report on official information and another to consider amendments to the Cook Islands Constitution. When their task was completed these committees were disbanded.

Each standing committee had specified terms of reference. CEC was required:

(i) to consider and keep under review matters arising in the economic and financial field including trade policy and the development and allocation of national resources;
(ii) to authorise or commit expenditure on the matters coming within its term of reference in excess of the financial authority held by Ministers and Permanent Heads;

It also deals with matters of regional development.

The Expenditure Committee was required:

(i) to review expenditure on existing policies, including the staffing requirements, and recommend changes in Cabinet where these are considered necessary;
(ii) to accord priorities for expenditure on new policies in excess of $150,000 per annum with decisions to be confirmed subsequently by Cabinet;
(iii) to authorise or commit expenditure not exceeding $150,000 per annum on new policies, including the staffing required, which failed to gain approval in the annual Review of New Policies or which were not included in that review, provided there are new and significant reasons to justify consideration of the proposal;
(iv) to determine departmental staff ceiling adjustments during the annual Expenditure Review;
(v) to consider and *either* decline *or* recommend to Cabinet any new policy proposal, including the staffing required, costing more than $150,000 per annum.

Of the thirteen committees, the five most important (CEC, Expenditure, State Services, Works and Legislation) had regular meeting times slotted into the weekly schedule. The other committees met when required. They could be time-consuming; one minister calculated he spent one-and-a-half days a week on committees.

The agenda for committees was determined by the cabinet secretariat, as was the agenda for full cabinet. The prime minister sees the agenda at the same time as his ministers. The responsibility for determining in which arena an item should be discussed lay with the minister promoting the proposal. If he wanted to take a submission to full cabinet, that was his discretion, within certain limits. As one observer commented: 'Cabinet does not operate according to a bureaucratic logic which holds that it should only deal with policy issues possessing a high degree of generality' (Galvin, 1982: 16). If ministers chose to use cabinet as a 'comfort stop', that was their prerogative, but they needed to develop an awareness if when they should consult (Galvin, 1982: 17). On occasions, cabinet then referred submissions to a committee for further review.

Formally, of course, the agenda of committees was the responsibility of the committee chairman, who was nominated by the prime minister; but that authority was rarely, if ever, exercised. Nor was the prime minister involved in determining what committees discussed, he was kept clearly informed of what was happening and could intervene (which was rare).

However the Cabinet Office Manual does lay down rules that must be complied with before the Cabinet Office will list submissions. Therefore submissions to the Cabinet Expenditure committee must be accompanied by a report from Treasury; those to the State Services committee need State Service Commission and Treasury reports, and so on (Cabinet Office Manual, para. E2.3). Also for some items prior consideration by a cabinet committee is mandatory; if for instance, they have implications for public service salaries (Cabinet Office Manual, para. E1.3a).

The three control departments, the Treasury, State Services Commission and the Ministry of Works and Development, play a key role in the cabinet committee structure because they have a basic responsibility for interdepartmental coordination. The Cabinet Office, which is essentially a processing and secretarial unit, relies heavily on the information networks of the three control departments in not only communicating the decisions of cabinet and its committees but for monitoring their implementation.

The main standing committees had varying but wide authority to approve matters finally without full cabinet endorsement. This was particularly the case in the CEC and Cabinet Works Committee. The Cabinet Office Manual states that

> each committee operates under delegated authority from Cabinet and accordingly has power of decision subject to at least half the members being present..., but where
> — there are major policy or financial implications
> — there is likely to be wide public interest
> — the Committee is divided and the minority opinion is strongly held
> the matter should be referred to Cabinet for final decision (para. D3.1).

The Cabinet Office Manual then states 'Cabinet committees are meant to exercise fully the authority delegated to them by Cabinet; otherwise the point of establishing them will be lost'. Here 'decision' does not necessarily imply cabinet approval, but rather a conclusion which includes recommendations to full cabinet.

All decisions of committees were reported to the cabinet at the next meeting under the item 'Reports'; but, although any minister had the right to re-open any issue at that stage, the purpose was for them to be merely noted. They were not there for confirmation or endorsement (Cabinet Office Manual, para. D4.1). The one exception to that rule was the Works committee; no announcement of its decisions were made until they had been noted by the full cabinet. Cabinet, of course, retained the ultimate power of decision and might require a committee to review its decision, but this did not detract in any other way from the committees' capacity to make final decisions with their full delegated powers.

There was however a difference in the way that the proceedings of cabinet and its committees were reported. The committee minutes included a summary of the discussion, although the points were not attributed to individuals. This record was useful as a guide for those who did not attend. By contrast there was no such detailed formal record of cabinet discussions. Apart from supplementary memoranda issued at the discretion of the cabinet secretary, the minutes recorded in self-contained terms the decision on each submission. Otherwise, the cabinet secretary kept a longhand record which might be consulted by ministers on request. (These longhand notes were regarded ultimately as the property of the prime minister.)

In most committees, the departmental officials played an important part. Up to three people from each relevant department attended to answer ministers' questions and that process 'sometimes develops into a flowing discussion with Ministers and officials all participating freely' (Galvin, 1982: 25). However, the officials then normally withdrew when the deliberative stage was completed and the decision stage was reached. The two stages were often distinct. In the Cabinet Expenditure committee, ministers proposing expenditure attended the committee and, supported by their officials, they put their case. But their officials were usually required to leave before a decision was reached. The Expenditure committee had considerable weight in narrow areas.

The main, and most interesting, exception was the CEC. It was one committee that must regularly make 'crunch' decisions. It was supported by the officials' economic committee which was serviced by the Treasury. Although it was not the only standing officials' committee, it was the most influential because its parent committee had widely delegated power. The Officials Economic Committee goes back to the early 1950s and it most frequently involved — according to subject — senior officials from Treasurey, Trade and Industry, Agriculture and Fisheries, Reserve Bank, Customs, Foreign Affairs, and Labour. It developed into a sieve for considering vital issues before they were presented to ministers. It was uncommon for ministers to put items directly on the CEC agenda. They were either referred to it by the full cabinet or brought up in a paper prepared by the Officials Economic Committee (Cabinet Office Manual, para. E2.3b). This process meant that the departments concerned consult and narrow any differences to the point where the issues for resolution could properly be put to ministers. It largely reflected a consensus with any options spelt out if officials were split on the recommended course of action.

During the CEC sessions, the atmosphere was often relaxed. In addition to the ministerial members and any coopted ministers, officials only attended according to subject matter.

> The meetings of the Cabinet Economic Committee tend to consist of a committee of Ministers discussing policy issues with a committee of Permanent Heads. In the process, the direct relationship between a Minister and his Permanent Head has become blurred. In particular, the doctrine that a Permanent Head should always support his Ministers on policy questions no longer applies here. In the seminar atmosphere of a Cabinet Economic Committee discussion, the Permanent Head is no longer obliged to follow his Minister as he develops particular lines of argument. Conversely, the Permanent Head is fairly free to develop his own point of view independently of his Minister once a question from a Committee member gives him the scope to do so (Galvin, 1982: 29).

The CEC was also powerful because it was the committee on which Muldoon, as Prime Minister, had chosen to participate very actively since 1975. When Prime Minister, Marshall and Rowling also played an active role in CEC. Muldoon was ex officio a member of every committee, but he attended only occasionally (as when, for instance, the Defence committee considered a large item). He was chairman of three standing committees that met when required (Civil Defence, Honours, Terrorism). He was a member of CEC officially in his capacity as minister of finance but not its chairman. No prime minister has been chairman of CEC since its inception. Where a Finance presence was required on other cabinet committees and the prime minister was minister of finance, the department was represented by the associate minister. In particular, the associate minister played a leading role in the Expenditure committee. As a result of the prime minister's participation, CEC could become involved in crucial policy areas which lie within the briefs of other committees. Besides, Muldoon argued that, while cabinet was the place of politics, CEC was sometimes a better forum for sorting out and analysing the facts because officials were there. Regular attendance at and participation in the CEC meetings also allowed the prime minister to meet and assess a range of public servants.

CEC was the arena in which many of the important policy decisions outside the immediate budget context were taken. It finally resolved items referred to it by full cabinet and made large allocative decisions at budget time. Observers, and some ministers, regarded it as a *de facto* inner cabinet.

Ad hoc committees did not have final authority unless it was especially ceded to them. As the Cabinet Office Manual states:

> 1.2 Cabinet may also establish from time to time *ad hoc* Committees for special tasks. Unless Cabinet specifically gives an *ad hoc* Committee a power to act it must automatically refer back to Cabinet. *Ad hoc* Committees of Cabinet may also be established by the Prime Minister; any decision reached by such Committees must be ratified by Cabinet.

6.3.3 *Membership*

The membership of committees was usually determined by cabinet on the initiative of the prime minister. After each election the cabinet secretary drew up a list of possible committees and their likely membership for consideration by the prime minister, who then submitted them as amended to cabinet for ratification. The proposals were generally accepted without significant change. Most of the time the membership reflected portfolio responsibilities and functional relationships. The inclusion of a minister was usually determined by the job he held but his seniority in the cabinet list or his significance in the party may have been the determining factor, quite apart from his portfolio. The CCPP, for instance, was identical in composition to the CEC with one person left off it. By one account, that was why it was created. Later other ministers were added to the list when positions changed or their status grew; they had to justify their inclusion by performance. But it remained in the prime minister's gift and some senior ministers never made it.

Membership of the CEC was sometimes perceived as closeness to the prime minister but obviously not all senior ministers could be included in it. Attendance at its meetings did give ministers some advantage over their other colleagues because they had a better idea of what was going on. If, however, items within their portfolios were being addressed then they were automatically coopted but that still left them outside most of the time.

6.4 **Conclusions**

In both Australia and New Zealand cabinet committees have recently been criticized because, it is argued, they have tended to detract from the collective capacity of cabinet. The general tenor of the paper by Roberts and Aitken (1980: 3, 8) is that in New Zealand the committees have led to a shift in the location of power and that authority has leaked away from cabinet to its committees, while among Peacock's resignation claims was the argument that by use of committees Fraser had attempted to replace his desire for the collective wisdom of cabinet. How true are these claims?

Committees are of course necessary and desirable as a means of reducing the massive workload that would otherwise come to the Australian and New Zealand cabinets. Because the processes and rules of committees are well-established and semi-public, it seems that their use has now become almost routine. The control of the agenda, for most issues, is not utilized by the prime minister; committee membership of the standing committees is determined as much by the initial distribution of the portfolio as by more direct manipulation.

Ministers in both systems are kept informed; they receive copies of all decisions and have the opportunity to review or re-open most of them, even if that power is not often used. Of course, they may often be unaware of the *reasons* for those decisions when the minutes are bare, as they are in Australia; to an extent that may lead to a decline in a feeling of the collective responsibility, but such a change is comparative only. Further the changes are mainly non-partisan. Committees have been introduced of necessity; changes of government may lead to changes in structure, but not to the acceptance of their value.

A mere ten years ago (in Australia) the committees operated far more at the prime minister's whim. The decline of the standing committees under Whitlam was one example. Now they appear to be better established and their importance is recognized. Prime ministers use them very differently; in Australia prime ministers have tended to achieve an overview of policy by chairing the important committees (Fraser) or almost all of them (Hawke). In New Zealand, with a greater number of committees, the prime ministers have chosen to participate fully on one or two (just CEC in Muldoon's case) in which the most important decisions can be considered.

In the Australian and New Zealand environment, it is worth remembering that control of cabinet may be achieved as easily by swamping cabinet as by limiting its discussions. If cabinet has a massive agenda, ministers have little time to prepare and well-briefed, capable prime ministers may influence outcomes more easily. The development of committees as an accepted and useful part of the process has probably added to the ability of ministers to participate more fully in restricted areas while possibly reducing the opportunity for broader involvement. If cabinet is to discuss the vital issues, then it must be able to delegate the less important to that second tier of decision-making.

Notes

This article is based in part on a series of unattributable interviews undertaken by the author in New Zealand in 1983 and in Australia over the last seven years. I would like to thank the participants for their assistance. This chapter has also relied heavily on books I have co-authored; I would like to thank my colleagues, Geoffrey Hawker, R.F.I. Smith, and Michelle Grattan because many parts of the chapter owe as much to their inspiration as to mine.

Observers of Australia and New Zealand have one other great advantage; both countries are much less secretive than Britain. It is possible to obtain in both places details of the way the cabinets work. In New Zealand the Cabinet Office Manual (published in January 1979 and amended in December 1983) has always been available to students of politics and since July 1983, when the Official Information Act 1982 came into effect, to the public at large. It describes the rules by which items come to cabinet and the form which they should take. In Australia the Cabinet Handbook (1983) has been published by the government printer and is on public sale. An earlier version (1982) has also been published so that it is possible to see how the rules have changed over time. There is no evidence to suggest that the publication of these details has done any harm to the conventions of cabinet government. It does of course make it much easier to describe how processes are meant to work.

1. Three sources were used in the compilation of these tables.

   (a) Dr R.F.I. Smith wrote a consultant's report for the Royal Commission on Australian Government Administration, *Australian Cabinet Structure and Procedures: The Labor Government 1972–1975*. This report contained figures prepared by the department of Prime Minister and Cabinet for the period up to September 1975. Table 6.4 is drawn from this data.

   (b) In 1978 there was a review of cabinet workload and procedures, undertaken by the secretary of PMC, Sir Geoffrey Yeend and his deputy. Although the report was confidential, the prime minister kindly released the supporting statistical material for inclusion in *Can Ministers Cope?* Table 6.5 is drawn from this material.

   (c) Since 1979, the department of Prime Minister and Cabinet has included in its annual report statistical details of the number of meetings, submissions and decisions of cabinet in the previous year.

Tables 6.1, 6.2 and 6.3 are drawn from all three sources.

2. Each year, usually in July, cabinet holds a 'budget cabinet' meeting. Cabinet first determines the general strategy, including the desirable size of the deficit. Then it considers each department's spending in turn. When officials between the central and spending departments settle on a figure for an ongoing programme, that 'agreed bid' is not reviewed by cabinet. Where they could not reach a suitable compromise, the 'disagreed bids' are brought to cabinet for final decision.

3. The section on New Zealand was completed originally in July 1984, in the weeks prior to the defeat of the National government of Sir Robert Muldoon. The new Labour government under David Lange abolished the existing cabinet committee structure (including the cabinet economic committee) and established a new one.

The new system establishes five 'sector' cabinet committees: Social Equity, which will review government policies on social services and justice, with the aim of redressing social imbalances; Development and Marketing, which is to improve economic performance and includes the supervision of CER; Transport, Communications and State Enterprises, which has amongst its tasks the review and evaluation of all state-owned enterprises; External Relations and Security is to plan for foreign relations and coordinate internal policing and civil defence; and Management and State Employment, which will maintain a review of the position of permanent heads of government departments.

Each of these committees will be responsible for expenditure in its sector. As well, there are three other committees: Honours and Appointments, Terrorism, and Legislation. The performance of this last committee is of special importance given the pre-eminence of cabinet in controlling legislative initiatives. A senior policy committee will have a supervisory role over the other committees. Its task, according to the official circular, is to evaluate major social and economic proposals and to achieve 'clarity, coherence and integration of policies'.

References

Cabinet Handbook (1982) Reprinted in *Politics*, 17(1): 146–63.

Cabinet Handbook (1983) *Cabinet Handbook*. Canberra: Australian Government Publishing Service.

Cabinet Office Manual (1979) *Cabinet Office Manual* (amended 1983). Wellington: Cabinet Office, Prime Minister's Department.

Crisp, L.F. (1961) 'The Commonwealth Treasury's Changed Role and its Organisational Consequences', *Public Administration*, (Sydney), 20(4): 315–30.

Crisp, L.F. (1967) 'Central Coordination of Commonwealth Policy-Making: Roles and Dilemmas of the Prime Minister's Department', *Public Administration*, (Sydney), 31(4): 287–319.

Fraser, J.M. (1978) 'Responsibility in Government', *Australian Journal of Public Administration*, 37(1): 1–11.

Galvin, B.V.J. (1982) 'Some Reflections on the Operation of the Executive'. Paper presented to the New Zealand Political Studies Association Conference, 18 May 1982.

Hawker, Geoffrey, R.F.I. Smith and Patrick Weller (1979) *Politics and Policy in Australia*. St Lucia: University of Queensland Press.

Jackson, Keith (1978) 'Cabinet and the Prime Minister', in Stephen Levine (ed.), *Politics in New Zealand*. Sydney: Allen and Unwin.

Roberts, John and Judith Aitken (1980) 'The Role and Influence of Cabinet Committees in the New Zealand Political Executive Process'. Paper presented to the New Zealand Political Studies Association Conference.

Smith, R.F.I. (1977) 'Australian Cabinet Structures and Procedures: The Labor Government 1972–75', *Politics*, 12(1): 23–37.

Talboys, Brian (1970) 'The Cabinet Committee System', *New Zealand Journal of Public Administration*, 33(1): 1–7.

Weller, Patrick (1981) 'Inner Cabinet and Outer Ministers: Lessons from Britain and Australia', *Canadian Public Administration*.

Weller, Patrick (1983) 'Transition 1983: Taking over Power', *Australian Journal of Public Administration*.

Weller, Patrick (1985) *First Among Equals: Prime Ministers in Westminster Systems*. Sydney: Allen and Unwin.

Weller, Patrick and Michelle Grattan (1981) *Can Ministers Cope? Australian Ministers at Work*. Melbourne: Hutchinson.

7

In search of unity:
cabinet committees in Denmark

Jørgen Grønnegård Christensen

7.1 Departmental autonomy

The truth about interdepartmental coordination is that Danish cabinet ministers enjoy a wide range of autonomy. Negative coordination is as important as positive coordination (Mayntz and Scharpf, 1975). What is and what is not to be brought on a common denominator is decided with the distribution of responsibilities among ministers. When some policy issues are grouped under one minister and not one of his colleagues, it has also been decided that these policies are politically connected with each other, and, by implication, that the need for coordination across departmental boundaries has been reduced for these policies. Government policy then is the sum of a whole range of departmental policies rather than one integrated and coherent policy derived from the overall goals of the incumbent cabinet.

This does not mean that interdepartmental coordination is without importance. Quite the opposite is true: ministers belong, after all, to the same cabinet and as such they aspire to present a joint policy to the electorate. Collectively, the cabinet is responsible to Parliament. So, in a parliamentary democracy, there is a built-in need for a certain minimum of interdepartmental coordination. However, because of departmental autonomy, ministers and even more their top civil servants give priority to coordination with the external environment of their department in preference to interdepartmental coordination (Damgaard and Eliassen, 1980; Christensen, 1983a; Christensen, 1983b).

Ministers have good reasons for giving priority to close coordination with interest organizations and public or semi-public institutions in their policy sector. They gain the support from this environment when they harmonize policy planning and policy implementation with it (Olsen, 1983: 148–54). Further, such coordination normally pays off a high political profit to the ministers and their departments. The ministers insulate themselves against parliamentary criticism for not having negotiated their policy with affected sector interests. What is more, through this form of sector coordination the ministers are able to anticipate threats to their autonomy as sectoral ministers, which might come from close interdepartmental coordination. In preparing, e.g., a bill which will entail increased governmental expenditure, ministers will frequently be able to present the Ministry of Finance with a political *fait accompli*, if they have mobilized prior support for their policy from interest organizations and institutions in the environment of their department. As for the departments, they gain stability and continuity in their external relations (Christensen, 1983b).

Under these circumstances, lack of coordination rather than coordination is the norm where policies conflict or overlap. At cabinet level ministers share a common interest in not interfering in the policies of their fellow ministers. By adhering to this practice they protect their own autonomy when some day they have to defend a policy which might not be totally in accordance with established governmental policy.

Nevertheless, there is an increased recognition of the need for stronger interdepartmental coordination. During the latest decade several initiatives have been taken to strengthen formal coordination and to expand the scope of interdepartmental coordination. This chapter deals with these initiatives. Interdepartmental coordination is presented in a broad perspective covering all forms of coordination. But the principal focus of analysis is the establishment of cabinet committees as instruments of interdepartmental coordination. Why have more and more cabinet committees been set up in Denmark during the last ten to fifteen years? What purpose do they serve when they are used? What can be said about their success or lack of success?

The analysis is based on a few rather simple propositions:

1. Contrary to sector ministers, ministers with a responsibility for general government policy have an interest in strengthening cabinet committees as one among several instruments for interdepartmental coordination. This is clearly the case with the Minister of Finance, but it may apply to other ministers with similar coordinative functions as well.

2. Alone, this is not a sufficient condition for the effective operation of cabinet committees.

3. Cabinet committees only work as effective instruments of coordination

(a) if, for political reasons, an issue calls for coordination at cabinet level, or

(b) if the cabinet is a coalition of two or more parties.

4. When the conditions set out under proposition 3 are fulfilled,

cabinet committees may relieve the cabinet of the discussion of certain issues, which otherwise would have been placed on its agenda.

7.2 Forms and scope of interdepartmental coordination

Coordination by cabinet committees is only one among several forms of interdepartmental coordination. Historically, it is even one of the more recent forms of coordination. It was not until the late 1960s that cabinet committees gradually were established as a normal form of coordination in Danish central government. Up to this time coordination was either referred to the cabinet or considered as a matter of informal contacts between ministers. Alternatively, interdepartmental coordination was dealt with according to more or less formalized procedures established within the civil service. Several instruments of interdepartmental coordination are in operation today. They diverge both as to their organizational forms and as to their policy scope (cf. chapter 1).

Basically, a distinction is made between two forms of coordination, i.e. coordination by a collective unit and coordination where a minister and/or a department are made responsible for the coordination of some aspect of government policy; the coordination of budgetary policy by the Minister of Finance and the department of the budget is the prime example of this form of coordination.

Coordination by a collective unit may take place both in the cabinet itself and in cabinet committees. A lot of interdepartmental coordination, however, is undertaken in committees set up within the civil service. In these committees members may exclusively be civil servants. But this is not the dominant pattern. In most cases these committees, which have increased in numbers over the years, will have representatives from both a number of departments with a stake in the subject matter discussed in the committee, and representatives from interest organizations and institutions operating within the sector (Johansen and Kristensen, 1982).

In committees with combined representation of bureaucratic and organizational interests, departments with overall responsibility for the interdepartmental coordination of an aspect of government policy will often have a seat too. This gives them an opportunity to get an early warning of initiatives which might conflict with general government policy. In theory, it also makes it possible for them to influence these initiatives in a direction they perceive as being more in tune with general government policy. Yet it is questionable whether they will be able to keep up with the massive sectoral interests which typically dominate such committees. Where coordinative departments may try to make the best out of an appeal to the general principles of governmental policy and even to abstract societal interests, sector departments as well as interest organizations can speak with the weight of very specific interests (Kristensen, 1980).

Most discussions of interdepartmental coordination focus on issues with a broad policy scope. Interdepartmental coordination and especially coordination at cabinet level is thought of as coordination of the broad lines of government policy. Planning of economic policy, employment policy, public expenditure and foreign policy are typical examples of what is considered as the main problems of interdepartmental coordination. But cabinet politics is not restricted to dealing with the grand issues of society. It is just as well a process where ministers constantly have to cope with minor, but intricate issues coming up more or less by coincidence, scandals suddenly taking the headlines, and problems without solutions which force themselves on to the political agenda and demand as a minimum some symbolic action from cabinet ministers. Interdepartmental coordination also deals with issues of this narrow scope, and cabinet committees are expected to play an active part in this kind of coordination (cf. proposition 3(a) above).

To set up a committee of ministers or civil servants represents an extremely flexible solution to interdepartmental coordination problems. No formal procedures have to be followed. The cabinet is entirely free to choose the kind of solution which it finds appropriate. A committee set up in one situation may be dissolved as soon as the situation changes, its mandate may be broadened or narrowed if that should be appropriate. When a distinction is made between committees with a more permanent status and ad hoc meetings between ministers or civil servants representing different departments, the flexible and informal character of the committee approach to interdepartmental coordination problems is stressed. Here it is without importance whether the committee deals with general policy issues or issues with a specific and narrow scope. In all these respects coordination by a minister and/or a department with interdepartmental responsibilities represents a very different solution. It is highly formalized, it is based on elaborate procedures, which specify what has to be done under given circumstances, and also who is entitled or obliged to do what. The high level of formalization implies that this form of coordination only represents a solution to coordination problems with a rather broad policy scope.

7.3 **The cabinet as a political checkpoint**

A concise characterization of Danish central government once stated that its guiding principle was its lack of principles. This is still valid. It is particularly valid for the status and the operation of the cabinet. The constitution contains no provisions for the cabinet. There are, furthermore, no rules of procedure for cabinet proceedings and for the organization of its work. No formal rules specify the role of the cabinet and define what should be discussed at this level.

Still the cabinet meets once a week. All ministers are *eo ipso* members of the cabinet. As junior ministers are unknown in the governmental system, the cabinet assembles everybody in central government with a political appointment. Although no formal rules set out what should and what should not be placed on the agenda of the cabinet, a fairly fixed practice has developed (Olsen, 1978). According to this practice the issues dealt with by the cabinet can be divided into three categories:

1. The cabinet agenda is highly influenced by the work in Parliament. So, without exception, all bills are presented to the cabinet by the minister in charge. The same is true with governmental proposals for other decisions to be made by Parliament; such draft decisions may be simple political declarations of intent or they may be proposals, e.g., for the ratification of international treaties. Normally, drafts of ministers' oral or written reports to Parliament and their draft answers to parliamentary interpellations will also be presented to the cabinet. Finally, the more general aspects of cabinet relations to Parliament are discussed at cabinet meetings. This is the case with the legislative programme as a whole before the annual opening of Parliament, and it is currently the case with preparations for and evaluations of negotiations between the cabinet and parties not represented in it.

2. Another category of cabinet topics with a fairly well-defined content refers to the internal organization and working of central government. Appointments of top civil servants (i.e. permanent secretaries and many agency directors) are presented to the cabinet. Proposals to set up politically more important committees are also placed on the agenda of the cabinet. This gives the cabinet the opportunity to confirm the precise phrasing of a committee's mandate, its proposed time schedule, its composition and especially the appointment of its chairman. When a committee has delivered its report, its conclusions will similarly be presented to the cabinet together with the policy recommendations drawn from it by the minister in charge.

3. The last category has a more residual character. It would not be possible to summarize its content. Further, its presence on the

cabinet agenda is not related to any established procedures or formal provisions. However, many discussions in cabinet deal with issues, often minor issues of passing importance, which for the moment attract considerable political attention and, therefore, force the cabinet to take position on them. They do not owe their importance to their policy content, but rather to their immediate or potential controversiality.

This listing of issues typically presented to the cabinet tells nothing about the role of the cabinet. But it would be wrong to see the cabinet as the supreme centre of coordination within central government. The cabinet is not a forum for the discussion of general policy. Neither is it a forum where ministers under the guidance of the prime minister lay down the general principles of governmental policy. The cabinet's role is far more to provide a political check on the course of government policy. Ministers present their cases to their colleagues to make sure that their policy does not openly conflict with the general course of the government and not least to make sure that prior preparations are adequate to protect the cabinet against unpleasant surprises when a minister confronts Parliament and the press. In this way the cabinet gets an important role in cases where the government feels a need to present a mutually recognized stand towards the political environment in a broad sense. This, at least, demands that ministers do not speak in public against the policies of their fellow ministers.

The cabinet is not the forum for lengthy and thorough discussions. The number of points on the agenda, on the average thirty per meeting, forbids that. But to this should be added the traditional reaction of ministers not to intervene in a discussion of cases which clearly belong to the sphere of competence of one of their colleagues. By paying mutual respect to this norm, ministers are able to put up a solid defence of their own departmental autonomy. When, now and then, a minister, be he or she stubborn or simply inexperienced, breaks this unwritten norm, he or she will rapidly gain a reputation for rocking the boat. Like the cabinets in Denmark's neighbouring countries, the cabinet, then, is neither a forum for policy discussions nor the real decision-making centre in central government (cf. Heclo and Wildavsky, 1974: 141–51; Mayntz, 1980: 143–56; Olsen, 1980: 135–239). The cabinet alternatively should be considered as the final checkpoint where some decisions of political importance are confirmed; these decisions have been prepared and decided elsewhere in central government. If it turns out that this preparation does not exclude disagreements in cabinet, a decision will not be made. Instead the issue will be referred back to renewed interdepartmental discussions outside cabinet. Given this restricted role for the cabinet in interdepartmental coordination, the question is to what extent the growing number of cabinet committees have a more substantive role in the coordination of governmental policy across departmental boundaries.

7.4 Cabinet committees

7.4.1 *Number and types*

Cabinet committees are a comparatively recent phenomenon in Danish politics. For a long period of time the economic policy committee was the only committee publicly known to exist. It was not until the late 1960s that cabinet committees were introduced as a general instrument of interdepartmental coordination. Since then a considerable number of committees have been created.

The sudden increase in the number of cabinet committees may partly be an artifact. Before 1971, the Prime Minister's Office did not produce any up-to-date list of cabinet committees. The reason was not the confidentiality of the information. The simple fact was that the secretarial services around the cabinet were virtually non-existent. Consequently it is difficult to get reliable information on committees in existence before 1971. Further, the distinction is not very clear between coordination in cabinet committees set up according to an explicit decision by the cabinet, and ad hoc coordination where two or more ministers negotiate a common problem over a series of meetings. The harmonization of central bank activities with government economic policy is an apt example of this. For years, representatives of the government were known to have regular talks with the board of directors of the semi-independent central bank. However, in 1977, when the whole system of cabinet committees was subject to a systematic reform, these regular meetings with a well-defined and stable body of participants were formalized as a permanent cabinet committee. This change in formal status did, of course, not lead to any change in functions.

Table 7.1 gives information on the number of cabinet committees form 1971 to 1985. From the table it can be seen how the number of committees has developed from one cabinet to the next. In the table a distinction is made between four types of cabinet committees depending on their varying policy scope. The four types are:

1. Committees responsible for general government coordination. For some of these committees, which have had or aspired to have a function as inner cabinets, the policy scope is as broad as that of the cabinet itself. But for most of these committees, the scope has been limited to a fairly general aspect of government policy, which is

TABLE 7.1
Cabinet committees by type

Policy scope	1971–3 Social-Dem. minority	1973–5 Liberal minority	1975–8[1] Social-Dem. minority	1978–9 Social-Dem.-Lib. majority	1979–81 Social-Dem. minority	1981–2 Social-Dem. minority	1982–5 Conservative-Liberal four-party coalition minority
General governmental coordination	4	4	7	7	7	7	7
Sector coordination	5	3	6	6	7	10	2
Trouble shooting	0	0	3	3	3	5	2
Specific case coordination	2	3	3	3	3	3	3
Total number of committees	11	10	19	19	20	25	14

Note: 1. 1977 figures.
Source: Prime Minister's Office. List of cabinet committees.

considered as being of importance to general government policy, but which can be confined to the jurisdiction of one or just a few government departments.

2. A number of committees deal with sector coordination in a narrower sense. Their responsibility is limited to one sector or sub-sector belonging to only one government department. A cabinet committee has, however, been created to make sure that due regard is paid to the interests of neighbouring departments or to the overall goals of government policy.

3. A third category of cabinet committees is of the trouble-shooting type. Their policy scope will, depending on the circumstances, be quite broad or narrow. Whatever it is, their aim is to coordinate government policy in an issue of instant political interest.

4. The fourth type of cabinet committees has a very narrow policy scope. They do not deal with general policy issues at all. They are responsible for implementation of government policy in the most narrow sense. In these committees a number of ministers make decisions in specific cases which for some reasons or another are considered as so sensitive that they can be entrusted neither to the civil servants of the department in charge, nor to its minister.

For some committees it is questionable whether they belong to one or another of the four types defined. So, the distinction between general government coordination and trouble-shooting committees is fluid when a committee is created with the aim to launch an attack on troubles as general as, e.g., youth unemployment. In other cases a committee may see its functions change over the years. Originally, the economic policy committee was responsible for economic policy. Sometimes it even had the status as an inner cabinet. For the period considered in this chapter, the committee is considered as belonging to the type of committees working with specific case coordination. The reason is that today the committee, although still in operation, is primarily acting as a clearing house for, e.g., appropriations going to be presented to the budgetary committee of Parliament.

The number of cabinet committees increased from eleven in 1971 to twenty by the end of the decade. In 1982, a few months before the defeat of the Social Democratic minority government the number had further increased to twenty-five. As the Conservative-Liberal coalition took over in September 1982, many committees were dissolved. In 1985 the number is fourteen. The temporary increase in the number of committees exclusively fell upon two types, viz. committees responsible for sector coordination and committees of the trouble-shooting type. Compared to them, committees charged with general government coordination and committees responsible for specific case coordination have, as a whole, been characterized by high stability. Of the eleven committees in 1971, seven still survive in 1985. Of these four belong to the type of committees dealing with general government coordination, and two committees deal with specific case coordination.

Among the committees dealing with general government coordination the committees for tax policy, EC-relations, government-central bank relations and financial relations with local government have survived from one cabinet to another, regardless of their political colour. A common characteristic of these committees is that they have been set up within politically sensitive areas. Tax policy, for example, has for years been one of the most controversial issues in Danish politics. A reform of the taxation system has constantly been on the agenda of successive cabinets. The existence of a cabinet committee for tax policy reflects the political importance of the issue. It is a forum for political discussions among the heavyweights of the cabinet rather than an instrument of interdepartmental coordination.

For other committees within this category, the interdepartmental dimension may be more conspicuous. But again, whether it is the committee for EC relations or the committee for financial relations

with local government, they owe their existence to the political importance of the issues on which they try to make out a coordinated goverment policy. So, participation in the European Communities never has lost its controversiality in Danish domestic politics, and the size and distribution of block grants to local authorities is one of the recurrent sources of conflict when, year after year, the cabinet makes an attempt to bring public expenditure under control. Similarly, the existence from 1975 to 1982 of a cabinet committee for employment policy illustrated how the arrival of a new political issue cross-cutting departmental boundaries was met with the creation of a cabinet committee which was made responsible for the political preparation of the government's employment programmes, the first of which was launched in 1975.

Much the same stability is found for committees of the fourth type. One, the economic policy committee, is mentioned above. Other examples are the committee for internal security, where a few cabinet ministers (Justice, Defence, Foreign Affairs, plus the Prime Minister) monitor the intelligence services and are presented with specific threats to government security, and the appointments committee created in 1977 to discuss the candidates for top civil service positions. The only exception from the stability within this category was the cabinet committee which could grant exemptions from a general freeze on public sector investments decreed in 1973. As these exemptions might have strong political implications at the local level, a committee of ministers was deeply involved in decision-making although the specific projects were rather unimportant from an economic point of view.

This stability is found neither for the sector committees nor for the trouble-shooting committees. In 1971 only four sector committees existed. One was the committee for private industry still in existence, another one the committee for housing policy, which for many was one of the hot issues in Danish politics. Then, in 1977 a number of new sector committees were created. The explicit goal was to streamline policy planning in central government and, in this context too, to strengthen cabinet control over it. With the addition of some further committees the number of sector coordination committees even increased to ten in 1982. Today, only two of these committees remain (private industry and energy policy). The reason was simple; most of the sector committees never were used for any purpose. They only existed on paper. Why they were set up and then not used by the cabinet, is discussed in more general terms in the concluding section.

Until the mid 1970s no trouble-shooting committees existed at all. Already under the Social Democratic minority government from

1975 to 1978, three trouble-shooting committees had been created. In 1981–2 there were five of them, and today, in 1985, two.

The creation of such trouble-shooting cabinet committees has a very specific background. They have been set up in situations where the cabinet has seen itself confronted with a demand for doing something, but where it has been difficult to do anything actively to solve the problems, and where no minister or department has been eager to take on responsibility for the resulting inactivity. A typical example was the creation of the cabinet committee for children's security on public roads. In a series of reports, one of the large Sunday newspapers had focused on road accidents where children were the victims of severe injury. Policy-makers were criticized for their lack of initiative, and then, in a final interview, the reporter confronted the Minister of Justice, responsible for roads and car security, and the prime minister with the problems. They had no other choice than to admit the problem, and, when asked what the government would do to improve the situation, the prime minister declared that a cabinet committee would be set up to look into the problem.

This may be an extreme case. However, the cabinet committees for alcohol and drug abuse, for immigrants, for weapons export, and for Christiania (a mini society set up against the law in a former military area in Copenhagen) were all created as a reaction to similar situations. After all, only the temporary cabinet committee dealing with negotiations on the North Sea oil concessions and the cabinet committee for youth unemployment seem to have combined trouble-shooting with policy coordination.

7.4.2 *Size and structure*

When cabinet committees were introduced as a regular instrument of coordination, their membership was restricted to a few ministers. The typical committee had three to five members, chosen among the ministers most directly involved in the business of each committee. Since 1978 these small committees have been the exception. Typical committees now have six to nine members, and committees with ten or more ministers were suddenly no exception (see Table 7.2).

With the increase in the size and number of cabinet committees, their internal structure has also changed. Today more ministers are members of more committees. Ministers with only a marginal departmental interest in the work of a committee may have a seat on it. Yet some structural traits remain stable. First, the minister most directly affected by the work of a committee will preside over it. In operational terms that means that the chairman of a cabinet

TABLE 7.2
The size of cabinet committees

	1971–3*	1973–5*	1975–8*	1978–9	1979–81	1981–2	1982–5
3–5	6	7	8	4	6	5	3
6–9	2	0	5	10	11	14	9
10+	2	0	2	5	3	6	2

Note: * Information is not available on the structure of some cabinet committees.

committee will be the minister responsible for legislation within the policy area in question. Second, neither the prime minister nor the two ministers with clearcut interdepartmental responsibilities (the Minister of Finance and the Minister of Economic Policy) will act as committee chairmen. For the prime minister the only exceptions are the committee preparing EC summits and the coordination committee together with its other inner cabinet forerunners; for the Minister of Economic Policy the exception is the economic policy committee and for the Minister of Finance the committee of public sector modernization set up in 1983. Third, ministers with interdepartmental responsibilities are represented on a great number of cabinet committees. Together with the prime minister they will have a seat on all committees responsible for general governmental coordination. In most cases they will also be members on sector coordination committees. For them a seat on these committees is a potential source of influence complementary to the bureaucratic procedures on which their interdepartmental responsibilities have been based.

Apart from these fundamental traits in the structure of cabinet committees, representation has varied a great deal over the years. At one extreme, there are ministers with few seats on cabinet committees (see Table 7.3). Several factors account for this. In some cases the linkage between their department and other departments is weak. This is the case for the Minister of Church Affairs, the Minister of Cultural Affairs, the Minister for Greenland, and for the Minister of Defence. That will often coincide with a limited political interest in the policies of these ministries. To this a third factor should be added. The Ministry of Defence may have few links to other departments. Nevertheless, defence policy is one of the ardent issues in Danish politics. Since 1960, however, multi-year agreements on the size of the defence budget have taken defence out of current political discussions among the political parties and thus reduced the need for political coordination of defence policy within the cabinet. For many years the cabinet

TABLE 7.3
Representation on cabinet committees

	1971–3	1973–5	1975–8	1978–9	1979–81	1981–2	1982–5
Ministers with interdepartmental responsibilities							
Prime Minister	3	3	5	8	10	11	10
Finance	8*	4**	12	14	16	16	10
Economic Policy	8*	6	12	14	13	14	10
Foreign Affairs	3	2	5	8	5	8	6
Sector Ministers							
Taxes	5	–**	5	5	5	5	2
Justice	2	2	3	6	4	6	4
Interior	5	3	6	11	9	18	7
Environmental Protection	1	2	4	11	9	10	11
Industry	5	1	6	8	8	8	6
Agriculture	5	1	3	3	4	6	2
Fisheries	2	1	2	3	4	4	2
Labour	6	1	8	8	6	11	4
Housing	4	3	4	8	9	10	6
Transport	3	1	4	5	5	6	2
Social Affairs	2	0	5	7	7	11	7
Education	0	0	3	4	4	9	5
Cultural Affairs	3	0	0	1	2	4	4
Defence	1	1	1	3	7	4	1
Energy	–	–	–	–	7	4	4
Church Affairs	0	0	0	1	0	1	0
Greenland	2	0	1	1	1	1	4

Notes: Ministers with temporary responsibilities omitted.
* From 1971 to 1973 the responsibilities of the Minister of Finance and the Minister of Economic Policy were concentrated with one minister, the Minister of Economic Policy and the Budget.
** From 1973 to 1975 the Minister of Finance was also responsible for tax policy.

managed these problems without a committee for defence policy. Not until the 1980s did the Social Democratic minority government set up an explicitly temporary committee for defence to prepare negotiations on a renewed defence agreement.

Representation on cabinet committees is not only a question of interdepartmental linkages and political centrality. The political standing of individual ministers is also a factor of importance. In 1981–2 during the last Social Democratic minority government, the Minister of the Interior was a member of eighteen cabinet committees. Only his personal prestige within the cabinet can explain that. As for the massive representation of the ministers of Environmental Protection, Housing, Labour, and Social Affairs on the committees of the same cabinet, this factor should also be considered together with the fact that, at this time, the cabinet was divided into several factions.

Political divisions of this kind logically lead to both more and larger committees. To have a cabinet committee with a broad representation of ministers looking after an aspect of governmental policy becomes part of the internal checks-and-balances in the cabinet. For a coalition of two or more parties this is even more important. In the 1978–9 coalition between the large Social Democratic Party and the minor Liberal Party that was tantamount to Liberal representation on all committees but, at the same time, to a Social Democratic majority on them. The balance between the two coalition partners varied from one committee to another according to its political importance and its departmental coverage.

In 1982, a Conservative-Liberal coalition of four parties took office. With four parties collaborating in a coalition this internal balance becomes even more important. This was especially the case because the four parties had a very different parliamentary strength ranging from the Conservative People's Party with twenty-six seats in Parliament to the four seats of the Christian People's Party (see Table 7.4). To this should be added that, for the first time in its history, the Conservative People's Party had surpassed the strength of the Liberal Party and, therefore, had a claim on the post as prime minister. The Liberal Party, however, was compensated with the prestigious posts as ministers of Finance, Economic Policy, and Foreign Affairs, while the Conservative People's Party had to acquiesce in a number of less influential sector ministries.

With this distribution of departmental responsibilities Liberal ministers secured a strong position in cabinet committees. The two junior partners in the coalition had none of the more prestigious ministerial posts. To guarantee them a part in all aspects of governmental policy-making, they were represented on all committees of potential importance. The Minister of Environmental Protection, who was the only minister to represent the Christian People's Party, got ten seats on committees, implying among other things his representation on the committee preparing EC summits and the committee for government-central bank relations.

In the summer of 1984, the Minister of Finance, who was also chairman of the Liberal Party, left the cabinet to become a member of the EC Commission. As the Conservative People's Party had nearly doubled their parliamentary strength at the January 1984 general elections, they now made a claim on the Ministry of

TABLE 7.4
Coalition structure and committee representation

	Parliamentary seats		Number of ministers		Number of committee seats	
	1982	1984	1982	1984	1982	1984
Conservative People's Party	26	42	8	8	31	39
Liberal	20	22	8	8	35	41
Center Democrats	15	8	4	4	15	16
Christian People's Party	4	5	1	1	10	11

Finance. In the following reshuffle in the cabinet it was agreed not to change the balance between the four parties, even though their relative strength was radically changed after the elections. So, when the Conservative Minister of Social Affairs moved to the Ministry of Finance, the Liberal Minister of Church Affairs replaced him at Social Affairs, and a Liberal MP was appointed Minister of Church Affairs.

This limited cabinet reshuffle had implications for committee representation. Because the Liberals lost the Ministry of Finance, other Liberal ministers moved into some of the central cabinet committees to keep the balance within the coalition. Since August 1984, the Minister of Energy has been represented on the important coordination committee, the Minister of Economic Policy got similarly a seat on the committee concerning appointment of top civil servants, and the Minister of Education was appointed as member of the committee on government-central bank relations. Apart from that the structure of cabinet committees remained unchanged.

7.4.3 *Functions*

Whatever the policy scope of a cabinet committee, its functions may vary a great deal. Often a committee will have two or several functions. Political circumstances together with the characteristics of the topic under discussion will determine what are the functions of the committee in a given situation. Over time it is further realistic to expect the principal functions of a committee to change. This happened to the economic policy committee. In the past it was for some time the inner cabinet. Gradually its status has degraded. For a decade or more its primary task has been the coordination of specific appropriations of political or economic importance.

It follows that it is not possible to say that a committee has a well-defined function. When the functions of cabinet committees are discussed below, the focus is on the functions of the system of cabinet committees as a whole. In this discussion the following functions are considered:

— policy planning
— inner cabinet
— mutual control
— cabinet relief
— policy implementation
— symbolic action

Officially, cabinet committees are considered as instruments of *policy planning*. They are the fora where a limited number of cabinet ministers, each having a stake in the policy area covered by the committee, have in-depth discussions of future government policies. Committees of the type responsible for general governmental coordination are expected to have policy planning as one of their principal tasks. As these committees cover sensitive issues ranking high on the political agenda, the level of activity is in most cases intensive in these committees. Exactly the same may be true for the trouble-shooting committees. They will in some cases have a similar policy-planning function on issues which suddenly attract strong political attention in Parliament or in the public, as has been the case with youth unemployment.

When a number of sector coordination committees were set up in 1977, they were ascribed a similar policy-planning function. But most of them never got any policy-making function at all. They demised from lack of activity, because they had not been set up as a response to any felt political need among cabinet ministers. They were a technocratic device which could only gain the support of the Minister of Finance. For him they had the potential of being an additional instrument of budgetary control. Yet, precisely for this reason, sector ministers had few incentives to use them. A review of the entire system of cabinet committees conducted by the Prime Minister's Office in 1978 documented their almost total lack of activity. As seen above many of them were by consequence dissolved in 1982, when a new government took office.

An important function of cabinet committees may be the *task of an inner cabinet*, i.e. as a narrow forum for political discussions between the prime minister and key ministers. As the inner cabinet, a committee covers all aspects of cabinet policy. Its task is not restricted to general policy-making. Any case, disregarding how narrow a scope it might have, will be brought up here because it is not mature for presentation to the cabinet or because the prime minister finds it too sensitive for discussion in the cabinet as a whole.

Most cabinets have probably had some kind of an inner cabinet function. With the lack of formality characteristic of Danish central government, the inner cabinet has sometimes been an informal group of ministers, often including the parliamentary leadership of the party in power.

On other occasions, a formal cabinet committee has been set up with at least the implicit status of inner cabinet. The planning committee set up in 1977 gained this status. Especially during the Social Democratic-Liberal coalition it became the place where the two parties either tried to reach agreement on controversial issues before presenting them to the full cabinet or sorted out issues on which they were not able to agree. Of course, they might be issues of general policy; often they were very specific issues which had given rise to conflict, first in bilateral discussions between ministers of the two parties, then at a later stage in lower level committees.

After the break-up of the coalition, the Social Democratic cabinet maintained the committee. For some ministers this was a cause of discontent. According to them it gave too much weight to the Minister of Finance and his quest for severe budgetary control. Confronted with this kind of opposition, the planning committee gradually sank into inactivity. The need for some kind of an inner cabinet remained. The 'circle', the nickname for a group of high-ranking Social Democrats, took over the function. In the Spring of 1982 the prime minister and his closest advisors, however, again felt the need pressing for a more formalized inner cabinet. To make the committee acceptable to the cabinet, its status as a *temporary* coordination committee was stressed.

During the present four-party coalition a (permanent) coordination committee has been set up with the status of an inner cabinet. Here a mixture of small and large topics deemed to be of political importance to the government as a whole are discussed among key ministers from the four ruling parties. During the first year of the coalition it seemed as if this committee was able to endow the coalition with considerable unity because of the four parties' dedication to common goals. With the 1984 general elections the internal balance between the parties was disturbed, and the coordination committee has since then worked much more like the planning committee of the coalition of Social Democrats and Liberals.

Mutual control is an important third function of cabinet committees. Even in one-party cabinets, this will sometimes be the case as was seen after the break-up of the Social Democratic-Liberal coalition. Political disagreements within the Social Democratic party were severe. Cabinet ministers publicly gave expression to their diverging views on government policy. In order to give everybody a voice on everything, the number of cabinet committees as well as their average size were increased (cf. Tables 7.2 and 7.3 above). By this move an attempt was made to contain open disagreements among ministers.

In coalitions this function of mutual control is even more essential to the unity of the cabinet. With the presence of ministers from all participating parties on all committees of political importance, it is guaranteed that cabinet level decisions cannot be made without the consent of all parties. Depending on the level of trust among the parties, the function will be more or less acute. In 1978–9 only a minimum of trust was present between the Social Democrats and their Liberal partners. Under these circumstances an elaborate system of so-called contact ministers was added to existing cabinet committees. Each minister was paired with a minister from the other party. The Social Democratic prime minister had the Liberal leader and Minister of Foreign Affairs as his counterpart. To take another example, the Liberal Minister of Industry had the Social Democratic Minister of Environmental Protection as his contact minister and vice versa.

The implication was the creation of a procedure where a minister from one party was not allowed to make a decision on an issue falling clearly within the jurisdiction of his or her department without the prior consent of his or her contact minister. If consent was not given, a negotiation had to take place between them. If they were still not able to reach agreement on a decision, the issue would be referred first to the relevant cabinet committee and in case of further disagreement to the planning committee of the cabinet. This committee thus became the final clearing house for many issues which had been blocked by the veto of a contract minister. The definitely minor importance of these issues giving rise to conflict between ministers from either party did not restrain ministers from using the system to block decisions prepared by a colleague representing the coalition partner.

For years cabinet capacity has been overloaded. The weekly meetings do not permit more topics to be admitted to the agenda. Nor would cabinet meetings leave room for in-depth discussions among ministers. In this situation cabinet committees have a function by *providing relief for the cabinet*. First, cabinet committees prepare decisions for later presentation to the cabinet. Bills prepared by a minister will today normally pass the cabinet committees in charge before being presented to the cabinet. The role of the cabinet is then restricted to confirm a proposal which from the point of view of cabinet policy has already been discussed at committee level. Second, cabinet committees relieve the cabinet of some work by making final decisions on certain topics. That is clearly the role of the cabinet committee on EC relations. As participation in the European communities is still highly sensitive, many initiatives arising from Brussels would have been brought to the attention of the cabinet, had it not been for the cabinet committee. Trouble-shooting committees relieve the cabinet agenda in a similar way. When over a long period Christiania, the outlaw society set up in central Copenhagen, was constantly focused upon by the opposition in Parliament, the cabinet had to treat the issue as serious. At many cabinet meetings it was one of the most discussed topics and therefore drawing attention away from other problems. When a cabinet committee was set up to deal with the problems of Christiania, cabinet meetings could be spared the discussion of a minor, but tricky and time-consuming issue.

As political chiefs of their departments ministers are deeply involved in current policy implementation. Ministers are personally involved in decisions of a very specific character, when policy is implemented. In most cases, these decisions do not involve other ministers at cabinet level. There are, however, cases where *current policy implementation demands coordination* between different ministers. As argued above, this may be the case if the level of trust is limited between ministers from different parties in a coalition. To this should be added the implementation of policies where even the most specific decision may give rise to political conflict. Export of weapons is such an example, where a cabinet committee was set up to deal with policy implementation in the most specific sense.

Governmental authorities are constantly confronted with a demand for action. Whenever a problem is discussed publicly, the question will be raised whether the government should do something actively to solve it or whether until now it has been sufficiently active in dealing with it. In discussions like this it does not matter that perhaps there is no solution to the problem or at least no solution which could be prepared and applied within the short delay asked for politically. Action is needed now and not next year when perhaps some kind of substantial solution might be cooked up.

In cases like this, governments take refuge in *symbolic action*. Then, at least for a while, they give the impression of doing something, and they have the hope that after some time the problem will perhaps not disappear, but then at least be repressed by new issues demanding public attention. It is generally recognized that organizational measures are often used in this kind of situation (Seidman, 1975; Szanton, 1981; March and Olsen, 1984). Setting up a cabinet committee is one of the easiest ways for a government to demonstrate that it has recognized the existence of a problem and that it has given high priority to instant action. The committees on children's security on public roads, on immigrants, and on alcohol and drug abuse all illustrate how cabinet committees have had this function. The establishment of these committees also demonstrates how the existence of a cabinet committee does not guarantee that this symbolic demonstration of the will to act is followed by any substantive decisions at all. After some time, when the problem giving rise to the establishment of the committee gradually is sinking into oblivion, the committee will be dissolved. This is what happened to two of the committees mentioned above.

7.5 Cabinet coordination and the civil service

According to Danish politico-administrative traditions, cabinet coordination was for many years an exclusive affair for ministers. No civil servant was admitted to cabinet meetings. The record of the meetings was provided by one of the ministers. After cabinet meetings no summary of either the discussions or the decisions taken was distributed to the members of the cabinet and their permanent secretaries. When a new government took office, the old cabinet kept its records as its own property. They were not disclosed to the successors.

The organization providing back-up for the prime minister was also weak. The Danish prime ministers never have received the secretarial assistance of an organization like the British Cabinet Office, the German *Bundeskanzleramt*, or the French president's *secrétariat général*. Nor does the prime minister have access to a staff of personal advisers like the French president's cabinet (Cohen, 1980).

Compared to the civil service assistance given to the head of government in other European countries, the Danish prime minister still is in a weak position. Yet, today he clearly receives more assistance from the civil service than was the case only a few years ago. In 1971, the Social Democratic Prime Minister Jens Otto Krag initiated a gradual reform of cabinet work. A civil servant from his office was appointed as secretary to the cabinet. His record of the discussions, which for all practical purposes is just a listing of the topics discussed and the decisions taken, was from now on distributed to both rank-and-file ministers and their permanent secretaries.

In the years following, the Prime Minister's Office was gradually strengthened. The intention was both to have a staff which could run the procedures surrounding cabinet meetings and which could provide the prime minister with some substantive advice on policy.

Still, however, the staff is limited to a handful of civil servants which aspires to follow the full range of governmental policy. There is, however, no doubt that today at least the permanent secretary heading the Prime Minister's Office is deeply involved in advising the prime minister on all aspects of government policy and cabinet affairs. Today, the permanent secretary will also be present side-by-side with the prime minister during most negotiations with departmental ministers or with members of Parliament.

The organization around cabinet committees originally varied a great deal. When the economic policy committee was set up just after the Second World War, a high-ranking civil servant was admitted to its meetings as its secretary. The same happened when a cabinet committee was set up to coordinate Denmark's negotiations on entry into the Common Market. For other of the early committees, there is no information as to the secretarial organization surrounding them.

In 1972, when Denmark took the final step to enter the European Communities, a high formalized and very elaborate system of interdepartmental coordination was set up. On the top of it was placed the cabinet committee on EC affairs. The Foreign Office department of foreign economic affairs prepares its meetings and its permanent secretary acts as secretary to the committee. To strengthen interdepartmental coordination on EC policy, a parallel committee of senior servants was set up partly to decide on matters not demanding the involvement of the cabinet committee, partly to coordinate the proposals later to be presented to the committee (Christensen, 1981; Ørstrøm Møller, 1983).

In 1977 a general reform of the system of cabinet committees was initiated. The aim was to strengthen interdepartmental coordination as a counterweight to the sectoral autonomy of governmental departments. The reform was inspired by the successful operation of the interdepartmental EC coordination system in action. On this background, it was decided that a civil servant from the department headed by the minister who presided over the committee should take part in its meetings as secretary. Further, it was decided to set up a parallel committee of senior civil servants for all cabinet committees dealing with either general governmental coordination or the coordination of sector policies. There is only thin evidence on the use of these parallel civil servants committees. It seems, however, that these committees have a level of activity corresponding to that of their mother committees.

The planning committee set up in 1977 as part of this reform was consequently also backed up by a parallel committee of civil servants. None of its inner cabinet successors have a similar parallel organization at the bureaucratic level. Still, it is characteristic for the increasing acceptance of civil servants as active participants in cabinet level coordination that civil servants from not only the Prime Minister's Office, but also from the Department of the Budget, take part in the meetings of the coordination committee. A similar pattern has developed for the centrally placed committee on public sector modernization which is responsible, among other things, for the coordination of budgetary policy.

7.6 The reform that failed

For years planning and coordination were the catchwords of administrative reform throughout industrialized countries. Through the 1960s and the 1970s more and more systematic planning and close interdepartmental coordination were the medicine prescribed for most evils hunting the public sector and making daily life difficult for ministers and their top civil servants (Schick, 1981).

In a report on planning in central government (Report 743, 1975) these problems were also identified as serious for Denmark. One of the principal proposals in the report was the establishment of four interdepartmental planning centres, viz. one for private industry, one for public expenditure, one for social redistribution (taxes and social affairs), and finally one for physical planning. The organizational set-up for these interdepartmental planning centres was proposed to be a cabinet committee for each centre assisted by a committee of top civil servants coming from the same departments as the ministers represented in the cabinet committees.

Contrary to traditional cabinet committees this new type of committees should not waste their time with the daily battles in government and Parliament. Their task was to force ministers to concentrate on long-range policy planning. To monitor the total system of governmental planning, including interdepartmental planning centres, a cabinet committee for planning was proposed. This committee should not go into substantive planning at all. Its task was at the highest level of government to follow governmental planning and to intervene when something went wrong. With these proposals it was thought possible with one stroke to overcome the sectoral autonomy so characteristic of Danish central government and the inclination of ministers to concentrate on incremental decision-making and politico-administrative detail.

When in 1977 the report came to be discussed in the cabinet, there was no support for a full-scale reform of the kind proposed. Among departmental ministers and their top civil servants there was a general feeling that some ministers would increase their status and that the whole scheme might threaten the autonomy of individual ministers.

In spite of this resistance it was decided to follow part of the proposal. First, the cabinet committee for planning was set up as proposed in the report. Second, it was also decided to reorganize the system of cabinet committees. Instead of the four centres for interdepartmental coordination proposed, a number of sector coordination committees were set up. The aim was to cover practically all aspects of governmental policy by a network of cabinet committees.

This system of committees never came to work according to its premises. The planning committee became the inner cabinet of the Social Democratic-Liberal coalition. In that capacity its functions became quite different from the ones stipulated for it in the report. Its members did not discuss the general themes of governmental planning which was its original task. Day-to-day politics occupied the minds of its members together with the problems of getting the coalition to hang together as one team of ministers.

As for the sector coordination committees they never got into action in most cases. The ministers chairing them had no strong incentive to bring their affairs to open discussion in the committees if they could avoid it. There was, further, no external political pressure for coordination across departmental boundaries on most of the sectoral themes.

Under these circumstances, which were fully recognized among cabinet ministers at the end of the 1970s, it is a source of wonder why these committees were continued, why membership in them was increased, and finally why more committees of this type were set up.

One tentative explanation might be that during these years the Social Democratic minority government suffered from a severe internal crisis. Ministers belonged to striving factions fighting each other as soon as an occasion for it came up. To set up cabinet committees to cover all governmental sectors and to deal with instantaneous trouble-shooting was one means used in this fight. When these committees were set up it could give the illusion of unity in cabinet, and ministers not trusting their colleagues were, at least on paper, given a voice on the policies of other departments.

In this milieu of striving factions the existence of the cabinet committee for planning with the status as inner cabinet met with opposition from some sector ministers. Especially the Minister of Labour and the Minister for Environmental Protection disliked the committee. They found that, with this committee, the Minister of Finance got too strong a say by constantly bringing considerations of public expenditure into the discussion. According to their point of view, it was impossible for them to fulfil their own political goals within these narrow restrictions. Their opposition did not lead immediately to the dissolution of the planning committee, but its activities were, as a matter of fact, brought to an end.

References

Christensen, Jørgen Grønnegård (1981) 'Blurring the International-Domestic Politics Distinction: Danish Representation at EC Negotiations', *Scandinavian Political Studies*, 4 (New Series) (3): 191–208.

Christensen, Jørgen Grønnegård (1983a) 'Political Bureaucrats: An Analysis of Bureaucratic Role Conceptions'. Paper presented at the ECPR Joint Sessions of Workshops, Freiburg 1983.

Christensen, Jørgen Grønnegård (1983b) 'Mandariner og ministre', *Politica*, 15 (3): 284–304.

Cohen, Samy (1980) *Les conseillers du Président*. Paris: Presses Universitaires de France.

Damgaard, Erik and Kjell Eliassen (1980) 'Reduction of Party Conflict through Corporate Participation in Danish Law-Making', *Scandinavian Political Studies*, 3 (New Series) (2): 105–21.

Heclo, Hugh and A. Wildavsky (1974) *The Private Government of Public Money*. Berkeley: University of California Press.

Johansen, Lars Nørby and Ole P. Kristensen (1982) 'Corporate Traits in Denmark, 1946–1976', in Philippe Schmitter and Gerhard Lehmbruch (eds), *Patterns of Corporatist Policy-Making*. London: Sage.

Kristensen, Ole P. (1980) 'The Logic of Political-Bureaucratic Decision-Making as a Cause of Governmental Growth', *European Journal of Political Science*, 8: 249–64.

March, James and Johan P. Olsen (1984) 'The New Institutionalism: Organizational Factors in Political Life', *American Political Science Review*, 78 (3): 734:49.

Mayntz, Renate (1980) 'Executive Leadership in Germany: Dispersion of Power or "Kanzlerdemokratie"?', in Richard Rose and Ezra N. Suleiman (eds), *Presidents and Prime Ministers*. Washington DC: American Enterprise Institute.

Mayntz, Renate and F.J. Scharpf (1975) *Policy-Making in the German Federal Bureaucracy*. Amsterdam: Elsevier.

Olsen, Johan P. (1980) 'Governing Norway: Segmentation, Anticipation, and Consensus Formation', in R. Rose and Ezra N. Suleiman (eds), *Presidents and Prime Ministers*. Washington DC: American Enterprise Institute.

Olsen, Johan P. (1983) *Organized Democracy*. Oslo: Universitetsforlaget.

Olsen, Søren Ole (1978) 'Regeringsarbejdet og statsministeren', *Nordisk Administrativt Tidsskrift*, 59 (2): 55–62.

Ørstrøm Møller, J. (1983) 'Danish EC Decision-Making: An Insider's View', *Journal of Common Market Studies*, 21 (3): 245–60.

Report 743 (1975) *Planlægningen i centraladministrationen* (Planning in Central Government). Copenhagen: Betænkning No. 743.

Schick, Allen (1981) 'The Coordination Option', in Peter Szanton (ed.), *Federal Reorganization: What Have We Learned?* Chatham, NJ: Chatham House.

Seidman, Harold S. (1975) *Politics, Position, and Power*, 2nd ed. New York: Oxford University Press.

Szanton, Peter (1981) 'So You Want to Reorganize the Government?', in Peter Szanton (ed.), *Federal Reorganization: What Have We Learned?* Chatham, NJ: Chatham House.

8
The Netherlands: cabinet committees in a coalition cabinet

Rudy B. Andeweg

8.1 The subordinate status of collective decision-making

The Netherlands cabinet started as an assembly of individual ministers to the Crown. Since 1849 the doctrine of collective responsibility gradually evolved to the extent that today a vote of no confidence directed against an individual minister would in most cases bring down the entire cabinet (Dooyeweerd, 1917; Van den Berg, 1981: 220). Yet it is only since 1983 that the Netherlands constitution officially acknowledges a 'council of ministers'. In the past, the only legal document pertaining to the cabinet was an Order in Council containing the standing orders for cabinet meetings (Hoekstra, 1983).

The until recently subordinate legal status of the cabinet symbolizes the relative lack of collective decision-making in Netherlands cabinets. Most of the ministers' time is taken up by their own department and an average of only 14 per cent of their working hours is spent preparing for and attending the weekly cabinet meetings (Gerding and De Jong, 1981: 78). In these meetings the debate often involves only two ministers (mostly the minister of finance and some other minister). During such bilateral discussions the others read newspapers or attend to departmental business. This is due largely to the tacit rule of 'non-intervention': to join a debate regarding policies in which your own department has no stake is frowned upon. In Parliament as well as in public, ministers are judged by their performance as head of department, not by their contribution to the formulation of cabinet policy (a contribution which, after all, remains a secret for at least twenty-five years).

The emphasis on the *Ressortprinzip* in Netherlands cabinets has a variety of causes that we can only briefly touch upon in this chapter. The most important factor is probably the segmentation or pillarization (*verzuiling*) that has characterized Netherlands society for so long. Until recently Catholics, Protestants, socialists, and to a lesser extent liberals as well, formed clearly identifiable subcultures, each with its own infrastructure of social organizations (political parties, trade unions, schools, media, etc.), isolated from and relatively hostile towards each other. In order to balance these centrifugal forces and to create some form of stable government, the leaders of the subcultures cooperated in what Lijphart has coined 'the politics of accommodation' (Lijphart, 1975). For the government to be acceptable to all pillars, the cabinet had to be a relatively broad-based coalition and the cabinet had to remain aloof from the daily political squabbles. In a one-party cabinet, conflicts between two ministers are likely to be conflicts between two heads of a department only. In a coalition cabinet interdepartmental conflicts can easily result in a rift between coalition partners (see for a comparison with the British situation: Van den Burg, 1971). The 'non-intervention principle' is designed to prevent such conflicts arising.

Secondly, the cabinet should be 'above politics'. This is symbolized by the fact that Netherlands cabinet ministers cannot hold a seat in Parliament. A more important consequence is that ministers tend to be recruited from outside professional politics, the selection criteria being experience and expertise in the relevant policy area (a professor of economics at the Department of Finance, a labour leader at Social Affairs, a lawyer at Justice, etc.).[1] This 'rule' has not been adhered to without significant exceptions, but it has produced rather technocratic cabinets. As a result, as former Prime Minister Drees put it, 'functional conflicts tend to be more important than political conflicts' (Drees, 1965: 25).

Since the mid 1960s the whole structure of pillarization has been slowly coming apart. It is more and more difficult to recognize the once distinct subcultures.[2] This development has certainly entailed important consequences for cabinet decision-making, but it has not led to a strengthening of collective decision-making. Now that Catholics no longer automatically vote for the Christian Democrats, or secular workers for the Social Democrats, etc., the proportion of floating voters has grown dramatically. According to conservative estimates, at least one-third of the electorate switches parties between two elections (Van der Eijk and Niemöller, 1984: 194). Whereas in the past elections were almost ritual occasions in which few seats changed hands, they have now become heated battles for the undecided voter. Polarization between the parties increased, not only in election campaigns, but also afterwards. The parliamentary parties now tend to see 'their' ministers as 'their advanced bases' in the cabinet. The weekly dinner meetings of the cabinet have given way to separate Thursday evening dinners where the ministers of each government party discuss the agenda for next day's cabinet meeting with their party's parliamentary leadership. More ministers are recruited on the basis of their political rather than their technocratic merits.[3] Depending on the coalition, political conflicts are sometimes of more importance than functional conflicts. Although this change is interesting in itself, both types of conflict continue to impede the development of true collective decision-making in the Netherlands cabinet.

The discrepancy between the doctrine of collective responsibility and the absence of collective decision-making places a heavy burden on other instruments for policy coordination. Since, in 1918, two ministers openly quarreled in front of an astonished Parliament, the prime minister is entrusted with the task of coordinating cabinet policy (Van den Berg, 1981: 223). For numerous issues in which several departments have an interest, 'coordinating ministers' are assigned: as 'coordinating minister' one of the ministers has responsibility for the coordination of, say, regional policy or international cultural relations or the prevention of coastal pollution, or consumer protection, etc. In 1980 there were sixty-nine such coordinating ministers (each minister having several coordinating tasks) (Vonhoff Committee, 1980: 239–241). The present cabinet has reduced this to fifteen coordinating ministers. Within the administration there are more than 200 permanent interdepartmental coordination committees composed of civil servants (Overzicht Adviesorganen van de Centrale Overheid, 1981). However, among the oldest and most venerable of all coordination instruments are the cabinet committees. To these we now turn.

8.2 Cabinet committees: an inventory

Next to a host of temporary committees, two kinds of permanent cabinet committees can be distinguished: so-called 'under-councils' (*onderraden*) and 'ministerial committees'. According to the Standing Orders of the Council of Ministers, the under-councils are committees dealing with 'parts of the general government policy'. What is meant by 'general government policy' remains vague, but it is interpreted as an impediment to the creation of large numbers of under-councils for matters in which only two or three departments are interested. The limitation to 'general government policy' does not apply to ministerial committees.[4] Eight articles in the Standing Orders spell out the procedures an under-council has to adhere to, whereas only one article deals with ministerial committees. In practice, however, the difference between under-councils and ministerial committees is largely a difference in name only, and henceforth we will simply speak of cabinet committees. These committees consist of ministers and state secretaries (or deputy ministers), but others can also take part in the deliberations. These 'others' are primarily civil servants or representatives from semi-governmental institutions, such as the Central Bank. Only three cabinet committees of relatively minor importance consist of ministers only.

A 'coordinating minister' is assigned to supervise the interdepartmental preparation of proposals to be put before the cabinet committee. For this purpose most cabinet committees have one or more so-called 'anti-chambres' (*voorportalen*), interdepartmental coordinating committees of civil servants from the relevant departments (see Kottman, 1975: 107–98). Some of these anti-chambres have become important institutions in their own right. The conclusions reached by the anti-chambre of the Council for Economic Affairs, for example, probably has more impact on policy-making than the languishing cabinet committee itself. The conclusions reached by the anti-chambre of the Council for European Affairs are sometimes put directly on the full cabinet's agenda. The anti-chambres do not have any secretarial functions: each under-council has its own secretary and assistant secretary.

TABLE 8.1

Cabinet committees in the Netherlands: an inventory (1 January 1985)

Dutch acronym	English title	Ministers	State secretaries	Others	Total
REA	Council for Economic Affairs	10	6	5	21
REZ	Council for European Affairs	9	2	8	19
RRD	Council for the Civil Service	7	3	3	13
RRDIA	Council for the Civil Service and Income Policy	7	3	2	12
RROM	Council for Physical Planning and Environmental Protection	8	7	7	22
AVR	General Defence Council	7	3	7	17
WR	Culture Council	10	8	3	21
RWT	Council of Science and Technology	9	2	4	15
MICONA	Ministerial Committee for North Sea Affairs	7	–	3	10
MCRB	Ministerial Committee for Regional Policy	10	4	1	15
MICIV	Ministerial Committee for Intelligence and Security	5	–	5	10
MCI	Ministerial Committee for Information Policy	4	2	–	6
—	Ministerial Committee for Policy Evaluation	3	–	–	3
—	Honours Committee	3	–	–	3

During the Second World War, the Netherlands government in exile in London first worked with cabinet committees (MITACO, 1977: 15). Immediately after the war, in 1946, the first official under-council was installed, the Council for Economic Affairs (REA), which is still in existence. Other under-councils came and went, such as an under-council for postwar reconstruction, an under-council for overseas (i.e. colonial) affairs, etc. Many of the present cabinet committees have existed for a long time, such as the General Defence Council (AVR), created in 1953; the Council for the Civil Service (RVR, now RRD), created in 1953; the Council for Physical Planning (RRO, now RROM), created in 1958; and the Council for European Affairs (REZ), created in 1963 (Van Nispen tot Pannerden, 1965: 232–3). Table 8.1 presents an inventory of existing cabinet committees.

8.3 The composition of Netherlands cabinet committees

All cabinet committees, except the Honours Committee, are chaired by the prime minister. This underlines the central role of the prime minister in coordinating cabinet policy, although this role is limited by the brittleness of the coalition and the prime minister's lack of formal powers. The official and the actual composition of the cabinet committees may not always be identical, since all ministers can attend, participate, and even vote in the meetings of all cabinet committees (this applies only to ministers, not to state secretaries and civil servants). The use that is made of this opportunity varies from committee to committee. In 1979 eight non-members made a total of sixteen visits to meetings of the Culture Council, but this is probably above average (Gerding and De Jong: 1981: 52). Nevertheless, the official composition of a committee is not without any significance. For a minister, membership in a commitee is an acknowledgement by the other members of the cabinet that his or her department has a claim on the policy area covered by the committee. The criterion for membership is therefore purely functional and not political. This applies particularly to the 'coordinating ministers': they always represent the department most closely associated with the relevant policy area (e.g. the Minister of Economic Affairs is the coordinating minister in the REA, the Council for Economic Affairs).

However, in a coalition government, political representation of the coalition partners in the cabinet committees has to be ensured. When ministerial portfolios are being distributed during the cabinet formation process, the effects of this distribution on the composition of the major cabinet committees are constantly kept in mind by the negotiators. When a coalition partner is satisfied with the

TABLE 8.2
Representation of departments in cabinet committees (1 January 1985)

	Chair	Coordinating minister	Ministers	State secretaries	Civil servants	Total number of representatives	Committees not represented in
Prime Minister	13	(3)	–	–	–	13	1
Foreign Affairs	1	2	4	3	8	18	6
(Development Aid)	–	–	3	–	–	3	11
Internal Affairs	–	3	5	7	>7	>22	4
Justice	–	–	2	1	1	4	12
Finance	–	–	11	1	2	14	3
Economic Affairs	–	2	8	5	4	19	3
Social Affairs	–	1	6	4	3	14	7
Defence	–	1	2	6	5	14	7
Education	–	1	6	3	2	12	6
Health, Welfare and Culture	–	1	4	2	1	8	8
Housing, Physical Planning and Env. Protection	–	1	7	4	5	17	6
Agriculture	–	–	6	3	2	11	7
Transport and Waterworks	–	1	8	1	3	13	4

Note: Development Aid is not a separate department, but only a minister.

composition of the cabinet as a whole, but not with the composition of its committees, new members are sometimes added. One of the most notorious examples is presented by the cabinet formation of 1952 (see Van Nispen tot Pannerden, 1965; Drees, 1965: 34–5). The composition of the cabinet had led to a clear overrepresentation of Social Democratic ministers in the Council for Economic Affairs. The Catholic Party objected and eventually the REA was enlarged to such an extent that today only two departments (Justice and Defence) are not represented and the Council is larger than the cabinet itself. The negotiations over the composition of the committees are often not completed when a cabinet is sworn in, and they carry on, sometimes for months, while the cabinet is already in office. As we shall see momentarily, political discontent over the composition of cabinet committees generally has adverse consequences for the role they can play in policy-making.

As far as functional representation is concerned, it is interesting to note that not all departments are equally represented in the cabinet-committee system. Some departments sit on nearly all committees, whereas others are represented in only a few (see Table 8.2). The central role of the prime minister has already been mentioned. The departments of Internal Affairs, Finance, and Economic Affairs also play an important part. The minister of Internal Affairs, for example, is coordinating minister of three cabinet committees; the department has a total of at least twenty-two representatives in ten committees. Internal Affairs tends to see itself as the guardian of provincial and municipal governments and may therefore show such a voracious appetite. Peripheral departments are Justice and Development Aid. The department of Justice, for example is only represented in two committees. Surprisingly, a mammoth department such as Health, Culture, and Welfare has only eight representatives in cabinet committees and it has no membership in eight committees.

8.4 Cabinet committees and policy-making

Officially, there are few restrictions on the activities of cabinet committees. They can address themselves to bills, money matters, appointments, white papers, etc. In practice, the committees are completely bypassed in one form of policy-making: the preparation of the budget. Budgetary matters are dealt with in negotiations between the department of finance and the various spending departments individually. When conflicts cannot be resolved in bilateral discussions, the matter is appealed to the full cabinet. As the budget is the principle — some say the only — instrument for setting priorities, the fact that the cabinet committees are not involved severely limits their role in policy-making.

A number of factors further limit this role. The Standing Orders make it clear that the committees have no status independent from the cabinet as a whole. The fact that ministers who are not an official member of a committee, can enjoy all the rights of membership any time they want to, has already been mentioned. Whenever a minister (member or non-member) so requests, a topic is transferred from the agenda of the committee to the agenda of the cabinet as a whole, even after the committee has reached a decision. Resolutions only become binding upon approval by the cabinet.

According to the Standing Orders cabinet committees can both prepare topics for decision by the cabinet and decide matters themselves. However, when one inspects the official description of the function of the various committees, they can only 'prepare' or 'discuss' proposals to be decided by the full cabinet. Only two committees, the Honours Committee and the Ministerial Committee on Intelligence and Security, have the authority to reach decisions (*Staatsalmanak*, 1984: B1–B6).

The role cabinet committees play in policy-making has not always been so limited. In the first post-war years the committees, and especially the Council for Economic Affairs, did play a substantial role (MITACO, 1977: 15). After the extension of the REA for political reasons in 1952, its importance rapidly declined. This is reflected by the drop in the frequency of its meetings (see Table 8.3).

Data on the frequency of cabinet and cabinet committee meetings are hard to come by. In the case of the Ministerial Committee on Intelligence and Security, the frequency of the meetings is an official secret.[5] In Table 8.3 we rely on data published by others. In the top row we find the frequency of meetings of the entire cabinet. Cabinet sessions sometimes take all day, whereas committee meetings rarely last more than three hours. To make the figures comparable we have counted each morning, afternoon, or evening that the cabinet was in session as a separate meeting. The most interesting development is the drop in the frequency of REA meetings after 1953. Apparently they tried to continue the role of the REA after its enlargement in 1952, but realized that it did not work. The waning importance of this committee is the direct result of the conflict over its political composition.

The 1973–7 Den Uyl cabinet provides another example of malfunctioning of cabinet committees because of flaws in their political composition. This government contained twenty ministers

TABLE 8.3
Frequency of meetings of cabinet committees and the cabinet

	1945	1946	1947	1948	1949	1950	1951	1952	1953	1954	1955	1956	1957	1958	1959	1960	1961	1962	1963	1964	1975	1976	1978	1979	1980
Cabinet	36	71	83	75	82	77	97	98	104	102	109	108	115	121	115	139	132	117	97	104		153		134	
REA	10	45	43	43	44	44	27	32	35	13	4	2	2	2	5	4	11	9	4	6			6	6	4
REZ																							4	5	3
RRD									3	11	9	5	9	9	7	6	9	6	3	9			9	10	7
RRDIA																							9	10	7
RROM														3	2	2	4	1	1	6			7	12	10
AVR								3	1	3	1		1	2	2	1	1	1	1		1	0	4	5	3
WR																							7	8	7
RWB																					1	1	1	5	3
MICONA																							4	1	0
MCRB																							4	4	4
MICIV	(frequency of meetings secret)																								

Sources: 1945–1964: Van Nispen tot Pannerden (1965: 235); 1975–1976: MITACO (1977: 16–17); 1978–1980: Gerding and de Jong (1981: 120–2).

and state secretaries from the three progressive parties (Social Democrats, Democrats '66, and Radicals) and thirteen Christian Democratic ministers and state secretaries. Van den Berg has drawn attention to the fact that the ratio of progressive to Christian Democratic ministers varied enormously from one policy area to another (Van den Berg, 1976: 229). In the area of international policy the ratio was five progressives to two Christian Democrats, and in the socio-cultural sector the ratio was 6:2. In the important socio-economic area, however, the Christian Democrats had the upper hand with a ratio of 6:2. As a result the cabinet committees played an even more limited role during this cabinet's rule.

Sometimes such flaws in the political composition of the committees leads to the creation of ad hoc cabinet committees. In 1984, for example, the Lubbers cabinet had to reach a decision on the deployment of Pershing II and Cruise missiles on Netherlands soil. All the ministers that had a direct responsibility were Christian Democrats. To involve the Liberal coalition partner in the decision-making process, the ministers of Justice and Internal Affairs were included in an informal ad hoc committee.

Although frequency of meetings admittedly is an imperfect indicator of importance, it is clear from Table 8.3 that most cabinet committees meet so infrequently that they can hardly play a role of much significance. Another indicator of the (lack of) importance of the committees is the attendance ratio. Gerding and De Jong present data on attendance at the 1979 meetings of three under-councils: the Council for Economic Affairs, the Council for Physical Planning and Environmental Protection, and the Culture Council (Gerding and De Jong, 1981: 50–1). Attendance at meetings of the Council for Economic Affairs was highest, but attendance by ministers and state secretaries at meetings of the other two under-councils was slightly over 50 per cent. The minister of finance, for example, was present at only three of the eight meetings of the Culture Council, and he completely abstained from participation in the RROM. The prime minister, the chairman of these under-councils, is not always present either: he presided over only two of the eight Culture Council meetings in 1979. It should be noted, however, that this may vary from cabinet to cabinet. The present prime minister, Lubbers, has so far chaired all committee meetings. This has a positive effect on the attendance by other ministers and on the status of the cabinet committees.

Apparently, civil servants take cabinet committees more seriously: according to the figures presented by Gerding and De Jong, the 1979 meetings of these three under-councils were attended by more civil servants than there were official civil service members!

TABLE 8.4
Opinion on the functioning of under-councils to relieve the cabinet

	Good			Not so good			
	1	2	3	4	5		n
(Ex)Ministers and state secretaries	12	64	8	12	4	100	25
Civil servants	54	38	8	0	0	100	13

When frequency of meetings and attendance indicate a rather marginal role for cabinet committees, it may seem anomalous that ministers and civil servants have a quite positive view of the role cabinet committees play in relieving the tasks of the full cabinet. The data presented in Table 8.4 are based on interviews conducted in 1980 by the Committee on Administrative Reform (the so-called Vonhoff Committee) as reported by Gerding and De Jong 1981: 48. One of the reasons for this positive evaluation of cabinet committees may be the fact that, perhaps because the committees cannot reach binding decisions, the proceedings of the committee do take the form of real and substantial debate. Compared to the highly formalized and mostly bilateral proceedings in plenary sessions of the cabinet, this may constitute a refreshing experience.

8.5 From triangle to pentagon

So far, we have concerned ourselves with official cabinet committees only. Out of a multitude of informal ad hoc talks between ministers who share an interest in some aspect of cabinet policy, sometimes more permanent coordination structures emerge, that are not officially recognized as a cabinet committee, but play an important role nevertheless.

Acts of terrorism in the 1970s led to the creation of a 'crisis centre' for the coordination of decision-making in the case of such an eventuality. This 'crisis centre' is usually led by the prime minister and the ministers of Internal Affairs, Justice, and Defence. However, there is no official cabinet committee, and no coordinating minister for dealing with terrorist activities.

The most interesting example of a pseudo-official cabinet committee is the increasing significance of a small group of ministers concerned with the formulation of socio-economic policy. The official Council for Economic Affairs being too large for efficient decision-making, the ministers of Finance, Economic Affairs and Social Affairs gradually came to form an unofficial cabinet committee, known as the 'socio-economic triangle'. As socio-economic policy became more and more the dominant aspect of government policy in general, the 'socio-economic triangle' became more and more important. For these reasons, but also for reasons of political representation, the prime minister joined the triangle in the Den Uyl cabinet (1973–7). It was then known as the 'socio-economic quadrangle' or the 'triangle with a head'. It was during this cabinet's term of office that the first criticisms were heard from other ministers, who felt relegated to secondary status.

The following cabinet, Van Agt I (1978–81), added a fifth member to the group: the minister of Internal Affairs. Political considerations may have played a role, since the minister of Internal Affairs was the vice-premier and leader of the Liberal party, one of the coalition partners. However, the minister of Internal Affairs is also responsible for personnel policy in the government-sector. Salaries in this sector have far-reaching macro-economic effects, and in that sense, there may have been functional grounds to include him. These five ministers became known as the 'Compass ministers', so named after 'Compass '81', the cabinet's socio-economic programme. The group met thirteen times in 1978, thirty-one times in 1979, and twenty-eight times in 1980.

According to the interviews reported on by Gerding and De Jong (1981: 36), in 1980 most ministers regarded the Compass ministers as a desirable development (see Table 8.5). Interestingly enough, the civil servants interviewed are less enthusiastic. In the official Council for Economic Affairs civil servants take part in the deliberations, and all meetings are prepared by the administrative anti-chambre. The semi-official Compass ministers had no official anti-chambre, and there were no civil servants among the members (although on occasion civil servants were consulted). The Compass ministers were not mandated to take decisions in name of the cabinet, but approval of their resolutions by the other ministers was routine. Some criticized this development as the first step towards an inner cabinet. The term 'inner cabinet' alone evokes strong opposition in a country where multi-party government has reinforced the doctrine of 'ministerial equality'. Not surprisingly, Gerding and De Jong's respondents reject the suggestion that the Compass ministers should form an official inner cabinet (see Table 8.5), although the civil servants interviewed have relatively fewer misgivings about such a development.

During the short-lived Van Agt II cabinet (1981–2), the criticism became more widespread. The Compass ministers were now called 'the pentagon'. In Dutch, this name evokes no association with warfare, but nevertheless the *vijfhoek* (five-corner) soon was

TABLE 8.5
Opinion on the development of Compass ministers

	Agree			Disagree			
	1	2	3	4	5		n
(a) Desirability of Compass ministers							
(Ex)Ministers and							
state secretaries	56	32	12	0	0	100	25
Civil servants	14	64	0	14	8	100	14
(b) Compass ministers as official inner cabinet							
(Ex)Ministers and							
state secretaries	4	24	8	20	44	100	25
Civil servants	18	9	9	18	46	100	11

nicknamed the *kijfhoek* (fight-corner). The pentagon became an excellent example of the difficulties that arise when functional and political differences coincide (see Tjeenk Willink, 1982: 13–14.) The Van Agt II cabinet clearly broke with the technocratic tradition of Netherlands cabinets. Most ministers were politicians rather than experts. In the pentagon, the prime minister was also the political leader of the Christian Democrats; the minister of Social Affairs was also a former prime minister and the political leader of the Social Democrats; and the minister of Economic Affairs was also the political leader of the third coalition partner, Democrats '66. The ministers of Finance and Internal Affairs were prominent politicians from the Christian Democratic and Social Democratic party respectively. These five ministers were constantly locked in conflict. The other ministers felt left out completely. They had to approve of all pentagon resolutions, but as the members of the pentagon were not just fellow ministers, but also their political leaders, approval by the full cabinet was a foregone conclusion. From what has been leaked in newspaper interviews, the original goodwill of the Compass ministers disappeared completely during the pentagon.

Yet, the present government, the Lubbers cabinet, reinstated the pentagon. Now that the prime minister is the only political leader represented, this pentagon is clearly of a different nature then its predecessor. However, the anomaly remains that the most important cabinet committee officially does not exist, and that the elaborate Standing Orders governing the official under-councils do not apply. No minutes are taken and distributed; the other ministers are only confronted with the eventual decisions.

8.6 Reform proposals

The system of cabinet committees has come under scrutiny as part of a wider movement for administrative reform. It is now generally recognized that in Netherlands political decision-making too much emphasis is placed on interest articulation and too little on interest aggregation. Coordination may not be a holy ideal, but a minimum of integration would certainly seem to be imperative. The need for true collective decision-making has become more pressing, now that policy-making is no longer about the distribution of increasing wealth, but about cut-backs and priorities.

Various committees, some of external advisors, others of ministers, have put forth several proposals to strengthen policy coordination. In 1971 an advisory Committee on the Interdepartmental Distribution of Tasks and Coordination (the Van Veen Committee) published is report. In 1977 an ad hoc Ministerial Committee on the Interdepartmental Distribution of Tasks and Coordination (MITACO) presented its recommendations. In 1980 an advisory Committee on Administrative Reform (the Vonhoff Committee) published several reports. In connection with its reports, this Committee commissioned a series of background studies (on advisory councils, decentralization, instruments of policy-making, interdepartmental coordination, etc.). Together, these background studies provide us with a priceless source of information on policy-making in the Netherlands, and we have made use of some of the findings in this chapter. To put some of the recommendations of the Vonhoff Committee into effect, an ad hoc Ministerial Committee on Vonhoff Affairs (MICOVO) was installed in 1981. The Minister of Internal Affairs was made responsible for administrative reform and a Government Commissioner for Administrative Reform was appointed.

To discuss the various recommendations made by these committees would be beyond the scope of this paper. Suffice it to note that gradually the emphasis shifted from technocratic reforms to political reforms. As far as cabinet committees are concerned, the proposed reforms all contained recommendations intended to give the under-councils a more central position. In its 1971 report the Van Veen Committee proposed, among other things, to reduce the number of participants (especially civil servants) in the under-councils. In 1977 the MITACO recommended that cabinet committees should be an official and clear description of their task, and that the number of such committees should be limited. The Vonhoff committee proposed the most far-reaching reform. Five major policy areas should be distinguished (administrative affairs, socio-economic affairs, physical planning, socio-cultural affairs, and

TABLE 8.6
Opinion on reforms in cabinet committee system

| | In favour | | | Opposed | | |
	1	2	3	4	5	n
(a) Reduction of the number of participants						
(Ex)Ministers and						
state secretaries	47	33	0	13	7	15
Civil servants	17	49	17	17	0	6
(b) Broader powers for under-councils						
(Ex)Ministers and						
state secretaries	40	45	0	10	5	20
Civil servants	23	15	46	8	8	13

international affairs). For each of these policy areas there should be one coordinating minister, one under-council, and one anti-chambre. All other permanent coordination structures should be abolished. This proposal led to several criticisms, such as the fear that the five remaining coordinating ministers would in fact form an inner cabinet. In many respects the debate on the five major policy areas resembles the British debate on Churchill's 'Overlords' in 1951, or Heath's 'super-departments' in 1970 (see 4.4.2). As of yet none of the reform proposals has led to actual changes in the cabinet committee system.

To give Netherlands cabinet committees the opportunity to contribute to the much-needed coordination of government policy, at least two reforms would seem to be necessary. First, the number of participants in cabinet committees should be reduced drastically. The average cabinet committee has between thirteen and fourteen members. Many under-councils are larger than the cabinet itself. Second, cabinet committees should have more authority. Interestingly, the ministers themselves agree with these proposals (Gerding and De Jong, 1981: 48–9) (see Table 8.6). A majority of the ministers and state secretaries interviewed by the Vonhoff committee were in favour of smaller cabinet committees with more powers. The civil servants interviewed were clearly less enthusiastic about these reforms (for obvious reasons?).

The main problem, of course, is that giving the committees more authority will create pressure to enlarge them. When committees have the power to take decisions on their own, the coalition partners will be even more keen on proper representation than they are today. The larger the committees, the more invertebrate they become. The experience with the REA in 1952 makes this abundantly clear. As the experience with the pentagon shows, cabinet committees cannot function properly as long as both functional and political representation dictate their composition. It would be interesting to study whether functional and political representation can be separated. The Government's Commissioner for Administrative Reform has recommended that the coordinating minister in a cabinet committee should *not* be the minister most directly involved in the policy area concerned (Tjeenk Willink, 1982). One could go one step further and construct cabinet committees as purely political bodies, designed to reduce the overload of the cabinet as a whole. Members would preferably not be directly concerned with the proposal under discussion in the committee.

This would be a drastic departure from the present situation, almost resulting in a non-departmental policy cabinet. Whether such a reform is feasible remains doubtful. The tension between departmental and political loyalties is an old problem in cabinet studies (see for example Daalder, 1963: 280–95). Hopefully a comparative study of cabinet committees can provide us with fresh insights, because cabinet committees have too much potential for the much needed coordination of government policy to declare them beyond repair.

Notes

1. See Dogan and Scheffer-Van Der Veen (1957–8), whose study is now being updated and expanded at Leyden University.
2. See for a discussion of these changes Andeweg (1982).
3. Between 1848 and 1967 only 35.2 per cent of all ministers had prior parliamentary experience (see Daalder and Hubée-Boonzaayer, 1971: table 17). Between 1848 and 1983 the comparable figure is 42.3 per cent (figures according to the Parliamentary Documentation Centre in the Hague).
4. Compare Articles 16 and 24 of the Standing Orders of the Council of Ministers.
5. According to Hoekstra (1983: 39) the Ministerial Committee for Intelligence and Security meets rarely.

References

Andeweg, R.B. (1982) 'Dutch Voters Adrift: An Explanation of Electoral Change 1963–1977'. Ph.D. dissertation. Leiden: Leyden University.

Daalder, H. (1963) *Cabinet Reform in Britain 1914–1963*. Stanford: Stanford University Press.

Daalder, H. and S. Hubée-Boonzaayer (1971) 'Kamers en Kamerleden'. Mimeo, Leiden: Leyden University.

Dogan, M. and M. Scheffer-Van Der Veen (1957–8) 'Le Personnel Ministériel Hollandais (1849–1958)', *L'Année Sociologique*, 3: 95–125.

Dooyeweerd, H. (1917) 'De Nederlandsche Ministerraad in het Staatsrecht'. Ph.D. dissertation. Amsterdam: Free University.

Drees, W. (1965) *De Vorming van het Regeringsbeleid.* Assen: Van Gorcum.

Gerding, G. and B. de Jong (1981) *De Politieke en Ambtelijke Top.* Den Haag: Staatsuitgeverij.

Hoekstra, R.J. (1983) *De Ministerraad in Nederland.* Zwolle: Tjeenk Willink.

Kottman, R.H.P.W. (1975) 'Interdepartmentale Beleidscoördinatie', *Bestuurswetenschappen*, 29(2): 91–111.

Lijphart, A. (1975) *The Politics of Accommodation: Pluralism and Democracy in the Netherlands*, 2nd ed., Berkeley: University of California Press.

MITACO (1977) *Rapport van de Ministeriële Commissie Interdepartementale Taakverdeling en Coördinatie*, Second Chamber of Parliament, 1977 session, 14649 nr. 1–2.

Overzicht Adviesorganen van de Centrale Overheid (1981) Den Haag: Staatsuitgeverij.

Van Den Berg, J.Th.J. (1976) 'Het Kabinet-Den Uyl en zijr politieke omgeving', *Civis Mundi*, 15(6): 224–31.

Van Den Berg, J.Th.J. (1981) 'De Regering', pp. 220–245 in R.B. Andeweg, A. Hoogerwerf and J.J.A. Thomassen (eds), *Politiek in Nederland.* Alphen aan den Rijn: Samsom.

Van Den Burg, F.H. (1971) 'De departmentale indeling en vertegenwoordiging van belangen in het kabinet — een voorlopige verkenning', *Acta Politica*, 6(4): 354–62.

Van Der Eijk, C. and C. Niemöller (1984) 'Het potentiële electoraat van de Nederlandse politieke partijen', *Beleid en Maatschappij*, 11(7/8): 192–204.

Van Nispen tot Pannerden, A.J.M. (1965) 'De Ministerraad sedert 1945', pp. 231–246 in F.F.X. Cerutti *et al.*, *Opstellen over Recht en Rechtsgeschiedenis aangeboden aan prof.mr. B.H.D. Hermesdorf.* Deventer: Kluwer.

Van Veen Committee (1971) *Bestuursorganisatie bij de Kabinetsformatie 1971, Rapport van de Commissie Interdepartementale Taakverdeling en Coordinatie.* Den Haag: Staatsuitgeverij.

Vonhoff Committee (1980) *Elk Kent de Laan die Derwaart Gaat, Derde Rapport van de Commissie Hoofdstructuur Rijksdienst.* Den Haag: Staatsuitgeverij.

Willink, H.D. Tjeenk (1982) *Jaarbericht 1983 Regeringscommissaris Reorganisatie Rijksdienst.* Den Haag: Staatsuitgeverij.

9
Cabinet committees in Switzerland

Ulrich Klöti and Hans-Jakob Mosimann

9.1 The context of Swiss government

9.1.1 *Introduction*

In Switzerland, cabinet committees have existed officially since 1970, although informally they were used before. Since 1978, they have been based on a provision in the Law on Administrative Organization.[1] Little is known about the committees and their activity. They have never been an issue in the political arena. Except for rare instances, they do not receive any mass media attention. Thus, at the outset of our study we did not expect far-reaching insights.

Our presumptions were that, comparatively speaking, Swiss cabinet committees are of rather marginal importance. Secondly, we hypothesized that their composition is not a politically salient issue, but rather a matter of functional appropriateness. Finally, we suspected that the small size of the cabinet and other particularities of the Swiss political system reduces the need for special intra-cabinet structures, thus relegating committees to only incidental relevance. To some extent, however, we found our initial scepticism unwarranted. There are committees which are far more relevant then a casual observer would have assumed.

This contribution is organized as follows. First, we outline the context and the organizational principles of Swiss government (9.1 and 9.2). In the main part (9.3), we analyse the composition and the working of cabinet committees. After touching upon functional equivalents of cabinet committees (9.4), we present some conclusions (9.5).

9.1.2 *Formal status of the government*

The Federal Council (*Bundesrat*) is constitutionally the 'supreme executive and governing authority'. It is composed of seven members who are equal in rank and power. The internal functioning of the Federal Council is treated below (9.2). However, it is important to note at this point that the Federal Council is regarded

155

and acts as a unity, internal deliberations and individual opinions of its members notwithstanding.

Federal Councillors are elected by both Houses of Parliament in joint session (*Vereinigte Bundesversammlung*). Their legal term is four years. Aside from the formality of re-elections after the four-year term, neither an individual Councillor nor the Council as a whole are subject to any parliamentary vote of confidence. In fact, a Federal Councillor serves for as many years as he or she chooses. Thus, vacancies are staggered and this is not a government of a partisan nature up for defeat or approval. By the same token, there is no reshuffling of the government after parliamentary elections.

9.1.3 *Political aspects*

The Federal Council is a coalition government of a rather special nature. Its hallmark is a unique stability. Ever since 1959, when the Social Democrats were granted two seats, the composition has been unaltered. The three major parties hold two seats each, with the remaining seat going to the smaller agrarian party. At present, these four parties control 86 per cent of the seats in Parliament. Thus, the Federal Council is practically composed as an all-party government.

Proportional representation and consociationalism emerge as key concepts for the understanding of the Swiss political system. The principle of proportional representation is respected in all elections to the Federal Council (at best, a contender may be preferred over the same party's official candidate) and it permeates virtually every aspect of Swiss politics.

Consociationalism (the *Konkordanzprinzip*), as opposed to majority rule (e.g. Homann, 1982; Rüegg, 1982), describes a mode of decision-making which attempts to secure the consent of all concerned before reaching a final decision. Therefore, the Federal Council's proposals and decisions usually represent some sort of compromise and they are hardly ever publicly opposed by individual Councillors. Furthermore, if opposition to government projects arises in Parliament, it often cuts across party lines depending on the specific issue at stake.

9.1.4 *Functional aspects*

The above outline suggests that the Federal Council is fairly independent from parliamentary pressure and party control. However, there are other constraints considerably limiting its potential influence. An active political leadership is severely impeded by the consociational principle, since any move beyond the management of routine problems is sure to offend some established interest. The representation of private interests in the political process is not only well-institutionalized, but also very effective. Many organized interest groups have to be reckoned with because they are capable of initiating the instruments of popular control. These are, for one, initiatives demanding amendments of the Constitution and, secondly, demands for a popular vote on a Federal Law (Referendum).[2]

A recent study on decision-making structures and processes in Swiss policies (Kriesi, 1981) notes as a further constraint the administration's advantage over its political superiors, based on its expertise in any specific area. Kriesi concludes that, to be sure, the Federal Council occupies a key position in the political system. Yet, its main role is to mediate and to integrate articulated group interests. Consequently, rather then developing and implementing clear priorities, it has to limit itself to little more than administration.

9.2 Organizational principles

The fundamental guidelines as to how government should be organized are, again, established by the Constitution. In essence, we can distinguish *two basic principles*.

As already mentioned, the most outstanding feature of Swiss government is the nature of the Federal Council's position. Decisions are always taken by the Council as an entity. Matters are debated and decided by the Federal Council, and the decisions are pronounced unanimously. Sessions are held behind closed doors and no ratios of votes taken are made public, let alone the stance of individual Councillors. This, known as the principle of *collegial participation* (*Kollegialprinzip*), forbids investing the President of the Confederation with any substantial powers over his or her colleagues. The presidency is an office held for one year by each Councillor in turn. with basically only formal and protocol duties. As a mere 'primus inter pares' the President is thus fully compatible with the principle of collegial participation.[3]

The administration is organized in seven departments, each headed by a Federal Councillor. Functions are distributed among these departments. The so called *department principle* (*Departementalprinzip*) implies that every matter is handled by a department whose head represents the issue within the Federal Council. Thus, every Councillor has a double function. As a member of the Council he or she is in the role of the statesman, partaking in the collective political leadership. As head of a department he or she presides over a branch of the administration. In some instances (e.g. Interior), these departments are rather heterogeneous conglomerates of Bureaus, Offices, and Agencies, which of course complicates the respective Councillors' administrative task.

To some extent, affairs can be delegated to a department or (for minor issues) to an Office/Bureau for treatment and final decision. This 'principle of delegation' is intended to relieve the Federal Council of matters of secondary importance. It is a necessary correlate to the Federal Council's governing function. Only if the Council is discharged from too many administrative tasks can it perform its duties as a lead-taking and coordinating government. The remainder of this chapter will investigate some ways of coping with this tension and of handling other demands placed upon the government as well. Cabinet committees are one option (9.3), but we will have to pay attention to alternative strategies as well (9.4).

9.3 Executive committees
This section deals with the historical background of Swiss cabinet committees, the policy areas they cover and, chiefly, their composition and functioning.

9.3.1 *Historical development*
Cabinet Committees are a relatively new phenomenon in Swiss government. In 1970, the official State Almanac (*Staatskalender*) mentions for the first time Committees of the Federal Council (hereafter CFC), then called 'Delegationen', later renamed 'Ausschüsse'. Of the eight CFCs listed in 1970, only one is marked as 'legally prescribed' (Railroad Matters). The other CFCs did not have a statutory basis at this time.

During the early 1970s, attempts at administrative reform materialized. Although other issues were deemed more important, the existence of CFCs was also acknowledged. Their function was described as preparatory and consultative, but frequently they suffered from the lack of a specified mandate (Bericht Huber, 1971: 20). The Administrative Organization bill (Bundesblatt, 1975: I 1453) proposed to establish a legal basis for CFCs and to provide information for the Federal Council through circulation of CFC minutes. It further intended to give CFCs final authority over matters referred to it by the Federal Council. Giving CFCs decision-making authority was contested and, consequently, abandoned during the parliamentary debates (*Amtliches Bulletin der Bundesversammlung, Nationalrat*, 1976: 1174). Thus, the Law on Administrative Organization (1978) only provides a basis for *consultative* CFCs.

9.3.2 *Policy areas*

The lawyers' debates notwithstanding, CFCs were in action. If growth is any indicator for success, the operation of CFCs must be assessed positively, for their number almost doubled. Table 9.1 illustrates the gradual enlargement and refinement of CFC activity.

TABLE 9.1
Committees of the federal council

	Year							
CFC	70	72	74	76	78	80	82	84
Railroad Matters	————————————							
Foreign Affairs	————————————————————							
Military Matters	————————————————————							
Science and Research	————————————————————							
Agriculture	————————————————————							
Transportation	————————————————————							
Physical Planning	————————————————————							
Energy				————————————				
Economy and Finance	————————————							
Foreign Trade						————————		
General Economic Policy						————————		
Finance Policy						————————		
'Jura' Affairs						———		
Federal/Canton Distribution of Tasks						———		
Mass Media								—

Of the eight CFCs publicized in 1970, three have been discontinued in the meantime. The CFC on Railroad Matters was no longer required by the respective law, and its subject matter is within the scope of another committee (Transportation). Its abolition in 1979 can thus be seen as an elimination of an unnecessary overlap. In 1978, the CFC on Economy and Finance was replaced by three more specialized committees. Increased complexity of economic problems may have forced the Federal Council to intensify and restructure its attention to this policy area.

The CFC on Jura Affairs was a somewhat special case. It related to the creation of a new Canton which concluded a longstanding conflict between the Canton of Berne and its French-speaking minority in the Jura region. It was dissolved when the final arrangements for this unique solution were made.[4]

Some CFCs are concerned with traditional government functions, such as Foreign Affairs, Military Matters, Science and Research. In

Switzerland, Agriculture and Transportation belong to the classical policy areas as well. Thus, all of these committees have officially existed since 1970, and presumably, they have been in action even before that year.

Physical Planning, on the other hand, is a new, not a classical task. Yet, by the late 1960s it became so important as to warrant a committee of its own. This explains the presence of this CFC as early as 1970. The creation of the CFC on Energy in 1974 can certainly be linked to the 'oil crisis' of the previous year and the ensuing heightening of awareness of such problems.

The CFC for Mass Media, established in 1982 and announced in 1983, points to the fact that the Swiss political system is still struggling to find legal solutions to the problems of monopoly radio and TV versus private stations, and to the host of questions posed by high-technology communications systems.

The Redistribution of Tasks between the central government and the member states of the Confederation (Cantons) is a theme which emerged from an increasing complexity of federal-state relations and from growing fiscal problems on the central level. As with 'New Federalism' in the United States, the key issue here is the distribution of revenues and subsidies.

In sum, CFC coverage has expanded in the last years, progressing from the more classical policy areas (e.g. Foreign Affairs) to relatively new tasks (e.g. Media) or to detailed attention to more specific areas (e.g. Foreign Trade).

However, when confronted with the complete list of policy areas in the official annual budget, several lacunae are apparent (Table 9.2).

Several reasons for the exclusion of a policy area from the CFC framework are possible. In order to merit the emphasis expressed by a CFC on the subject, an area should exhibit a need for interdepartmental coordination or be the object of substantive policy-making of some consequence. Several areas in the Annual Budget's listing are either purely administrative (1, 2, 4), or of minor substantial importance (3, 15, 16), or they are entirely within the realm of one department (2, 3, 15, 16).

There is, however, an entire block of policy areas (7–11) which concern more than one department and are substantively important. There are two plausible reasons for the lack of CFCs in these areas. The principally concerned offices for the respective tasks are all within the Department of Interior. Although this does not mean that there are no other departments potentially involved, it is possible that most coordinating efforts are handled within or by the department. Since Interior is the most heterogeneous of all

TABLE 9.2
Coverage of CFCs

Policy areas (% share in 1982 budget)	Committee of the Federal Council
1 Authorities, Gen. Administration (3.1)	——
2 Administration of Justice (0.8)	——
3 Police (0.2)	——
4 Special Services (0.5)	——
5 Foreign Relations (4.3)	Foreign Affairs
	⎰ Foreign Trade
6 National Defence (21.1)	⎱ Military Matters
7 Education and Research (8.5)	Science and Research
8 Culture, Recreation and Sports (0.6)	——
9 Public Health (0.2)	——
10 Environmental Protection (0.8)	——
11 Social Welfare (22.3)	——
12 Physical Planning/Regional Development (0.3)	Physical Planning
13 Transportation and Energy (15.3)	⎰ Transportation
	⎱ Energy
14 Agriculture and Nutrition (7.9)	Agriculture
15 Forestry, Hunting and Fishing (0.2)	——
16 Waters Correction and Avalanche Protection (0.3)	——
17 Industry, Trade and Crafts (0.3)	General Economic Policy
18 Finance (13.3)	Finance Policy
–	Jura Affairs
–	Federal/Canton Distribution of Tasks
–	Mass Media

departments, it is likely that it can rely on more longstanding experience with such procedures. Another explanation would be more personalized: since a CFC is usually created on the initiative of the most concerned department head, it is conceivable that the relevant Federal Councillor did not *wnat* an official interdepartmental stage created for these issues.

9.3.3 *Composition of CFCs*

Introduction. CFCs invariably consist of three Federal Councillors. In comparison with other countries, then, Swiss cabinet committees are extremely small. Furthermore, there is little freedom of manoeuvre for representational purposes. With only three positions to be occupied, one cannot satisfy the four coalition parties at one and the same time, let alone represent them proportionally.

The main question asked in this section is whether substantive or political criteria determine the composition of CFCs. If substantive criteria prevail, CFCs will include the heads of the most involved departments, and the departmental composition will remain stable despite personal changes at the top of some departments. If political considerations dominate, the partisan and linguistic provenance of Federal Councillors will be balanced in proportional representation, regardless of the substantive competence of the departments thus present in a CFC.

The departmental composition is displayed in Appendix 9.2 (together with a glossary of the departments' abbreviations). Two facts strike the eye. First, the *chair* of every CFC remains constantly with the same department, and — even more telling — this is always the department which is the most concerned. Second, the departmental composition of $^3/_5$ of the CFCs is perfectly stable. Therefore, we will first present the stable CFCs, and will then treat those with changes of the departments represented. For the latter, potential reasons (substantive and political) for the changes are examined.

Stable Committees. The CFC on Railroad Matters was chaired by the head of the Department of Transportation and Energy (EVED). The policy area certainly touches upon financial questions, for Swiss railroads are state-owned — thus the Department of Finance (EFD) is involved. Situated in the heart of Europe, Switzerland is an important land of transit. This entails a need for international consultation and for legal agreements with the bordering countries, justifying the inclusion of the Department of Foreign Affairs (EDA). In sum, the composition of the CFC on Railroad Matters can be explained on exclusively substantive grounds.

The chair of the CFC on Science and Research is taken by the Department of the Interior (EDI) which houses the corresponding Office of Education and Science. To compensate for the lack of natural resources, the Swiss economy relies heavily on processing and finishing, and on a specialized services sector. Education and research are, therefore, of chief economic importance, warranting the inclusion of the Department of Economy (EVD). Switzerland is dependent on extensive exchange and presence in the appropriate international organizations in this field too, thus the EDA is represented as well.

For obvious reasons, the CFC on Energy is chaired by the

EVED. The economic relevance of energy problems accounts for the presence of the EVD. Interior (EDI), finally, houses the Office for Environmental Protection.

Economy and Finance, the CFC replaced by three more specialized committees after 1977, relates foremost to the Department of Economy (EVD), as well as to the Department of Finance (EFD). The presence of the EDA is explained by the high degree of economic interdependence and the importance of international organizations in this field. The same reasoning applies to the later CFC on Foreign Trade, formed by the same departments.

The CFCs on Jura Affairs and on the Federal/Canton Distribution of Tasks are identically composed. The chair goes to Justice (EJPD), for in both areas legal questions are of paramount importance. Financial aspects (revenue sharing) explain the presence of the EFD in the CFC on Distribution of Tasks, but less so in the Jura Affairs committee. No substantive reason, finally, appears for the inclusion of the Department of Military Affairs (EMD). Here, representational considerations are likely, for both issues are politically more sensitive than some routine policy areas. Furthermore, both CFCs are concerned with tasks of limited duration rather than permanent state functions. In 1980, the EJPD was headed by a German-speaking Christian Democrat. Of the two Social Democrats, one (French-speaking) was at the EDA, a most ill-suited department for both issues. The other Social Democrat (German-speaking) headed Finance, which in one instance was even an appropriate department. The third position, finally, should be taken by a (possibly French-speaking) Radical Democrat (the third major party). This Councillor was, and still is, head of the EMD. This, then, explains the surprising presence of the military in both CFCs. On last point has to be made: after the election of two new Councillors for 1983, the departmental composition of the two CFCs in question remained the same, although the EJPD, formerly headed by a Christian Democrat, was now run by a Radical Democrat. This indicates that, although concessions to proportional representation are made in the composition of these CFCs, they do not supersede substantive considerations.

The new CFC on Mass Media is headed by the department which up to now has been the only federal authority with some technical responsibilities for these matters (EVED). Justice (EJPD) is involved because the key issues revolve around the creation and implementation of an acceptable constitutional framework. The inclusion of Interior (EDI) is due to its housing the Office of Cultural Affairs, responsible among other things for the promotion of film-making.

Changes in departmental composition. Here, we present the six CFCs where the composition has changed over time (once in two cases, twice in four). Of ten changes, seven occurred at the occasion of major rotations (1973–4: three; 1982–3: four). These rotations are analysed separately below.

The CFC on Foreign Affairs was chaired continuously by the appropriate department (EDA). The uninterrupted presence of the Department of Economy (EVD) is attributable to the substantive interrelation between foreign policy and the export economy. In 1974, the third position in the CFC went from the EFD to the EJPD. Since the heads of all departments involved were the same in 1973 and 1974, the reason must be a substantive one. The increased importance of bi- and multilateral treaties (without a comparable expansion in the financial realm) might justify the change of departments involved.

The chair of the CFC on Military Matters goes, of course, to the department head of the EMD. Since national defence is a costly undertaking, the second position has been continuously taken by the EFD. The changes in the third position are less obvious on a substantive level (from EVED to EJPD and to EVD, cf. Appendix 9.1, Table 1).

Agriculture is primarily handled by the EVD which consequently chaired the corresponding CFC throughout the period. The sector is heavily subsidized and the fields of Alcohol and Grain are handled by the Finance Department, hence the presence of the EFD. The changes in the third position (from EJPD to EDI and to EMD) are displayed in Table 2, Appendix 9.2.

The composition of the CFC on Transportation has remained unaltered for almost fourteen years. Chaired by the appropriate department (EVED), it was composed of the head of the department of Justice and Police (EJPD), so that the legal aspects (e.g. traffic regulations) were represented, and by the department managing the construction of interstate highways (EDI). However, in Autumn 1984, the third seat changed from the EDI to the Department of Finances (EFD), when after a by-election the CFCs were reassigned. Yet, no changes occurred in any other CFC, which indicates a potential substantive reason for the change in question: highway construction is declining in importance, whereas the financial aspects are becoming more prominent, such as the deficit of the federal railways or the use of taxes on gasoline for environmental purposes. At the same time, the office responsible for the constuction of highways was transferred from Interior to Energy and Transportation (EVED).

In Switzerland, Physical Planning is foremost an affair of legal nature. As expected, the relevant CFC was continuously chaired by the Department of Justice (EJPD) which houses the relevant office. The remaining two seats, however, have changed twice among three departments (see Table 9.3). In substantive terms, all three departments are certainly more concerned with the policy area in question than those never present in this CFC (EDA, EMD, EFD). Between them. there is no compelling motive for inclusion or omission. Yet, the change in 1978/9 cannot be due to political concerns since none of the department heads changed at this time.

TABLE 9.3
CFC on physical planning: second and third seat

Department	Year					
	70	73	74	78	79	84
EVD	————————————————————					
EDI	—————————			—————————		
EVED			———————————————————			

The CFC on General Economic Policy has always been chaired by the appropriate Department (EVD). The uninterrupted presence of the EFD is also consistent with the nature of the policy area. The change in the third position from EJPD to EMD in 1982/3 has to be seen in the context of the rotation at this time (discussed below), because there is no apparent substantive interpretation at hand.

The CFC on Finance Policy shows a considerable fluctuation. The chair, understandably, always remained with the EFD. The second position was, also invariably, taken by the EDI. The third position has changed as shown in Table 3, Appendix 9.1.

Both the inclusion of the EMD in 1979/80 and the subsequent shift to the EJPD (1982/3) elude a substantive interpretation. Besides the rotation perspective (discussed below), there is a possible political interpretation. Given the fiscal problems on the federal level, this CFC deals with a politically very sensitive issue, entailing a certain need for partisan and linguistic balance. To examine this proportion we present Table 9.4.

Several explanatory aspects appear in this table. First, the presence of the EDI may be due to the need for a Christian Democrat. Second, in 1980 several departments changed heads. With the Social Democrat heading the EFD, there was a need for a

TABLE 9.4

CFC on finance policy: composition

	–1979	1980–2	1983
Chair (EFD)	FDP, f	SP, g	SP, g
2. (EDI)	CVP, g	CVP, g	CVP, g
3. (several)	SP, g	FDP, f	FDP, g

Notes: FDP: Radical Democrat
  CVP: Christian Democrat
  SP: Social Democrat
  g: German-speaking
  f: French- (Italian-) speaking

(possibly French-speaking) Radical Democrat on the third seat. This Councillor was head of the EMD, which explains the military presence in representational terms. The representation of the three major parties continues in the 1983 composition, after another change of some departments into new hands.

Rotations 1973–4 and 1982–3. Since we could not identify compelling substantive reasons for some changes in the departmental composition, this section is concerned with indications for political motivations underlying the two rotations.

From 1973 to 1974, the departmental composition of three CFCs changed. Table 9.5 sums up the political dimensions of this rotation. The chairmen of all three CFCs remained the same individual Councillors. This already indicates that the changes, although they did occur, were not far-reaching. The breakdown by party and by language quite clearly shows that in this respect nothing really changed (except for the slight shift toward the German-speaking majority). Since even the share of positions by each department involved remained the same, there is no convincing explanation in terms of our analytical categories. One might consider the individual ambitions and interests of the Councillors involved, but this, of course, is speculation. We must *conclude* that the rotation of 1973/4 cannot be attributed to either substantive or political motives.

From 1982–3, the all-time record of four changes in the departmental composition occurred. Table 9.6 outlines the political dimensions of the composition of all CFCs in 1982 and 1983. Again, the changes are close to invisible. The slight alteration in the distribution of chairman positions is due to the creation of the CFC on Mass Media. This chair is allocated on substantive grounds to the head of the EVED (an agrarian). The change in the overall

TABLE 9.5
Rotation 1973–4

	1973 (%)	1974 (%)
Chairmen	identical	
Seats by party:		
FDP	4	4
CVP	3	3
SP	1	1
SVP*	1	1
by language:		
French/It.	3 (33)	2 (22)
German	6 (67)	7 (78)

Note: * SVP: Swiss People's Party (agrarian).

TABLE 9.6
CFC Composition 1982–3

	1982 (%)	1983 (%)
Chair		
— by department	identical	
— by party:		
FDP	4	4
CVP	4	4
SP	2	2
SVP	2	3
— by language:		
French	2 (17)	2 (15)
German	10 (83)	11 (85)
Seats		
— by party:		
FDP	10 (28)	10 (26)
CVP	13 (36)	15 (38)
SP	10 (28)	10 (26)
SVP	3 (8)	4 (10)
Total	36 100	39 100
— by language:		
French	7 (19)	8 (21)
German	29 (81)	31 (79)
Total	36 100	39 100

composition was caused by the creation of the new committee and was insignificant. By the same token, then, the rotation of departments in four CFCs is not stimulated by political motives. The over-representation of the Christian Democrats (CVP) in the overall distribution indicates that the composition of individual CFCs is not intended to produce the otherwise well-known strictly proportional parcelling-out of positions.

Considering the overwhelming amount of stability in the departmental composition, the lack of detectable political intentions behind those few changes which cannot be explained substantively, the near perfect fit of CFC policy area and departments present, and the absolute continuity in the attribution of CFC chairs to the most appropriate department head, a conclusion is warranted: the composition of CFCs is based almost exclusively on substantive grounds. Considerations of partisan and linguistic representation do not have any noticeable influence, save for a few politically very sensitive policy areas (Finance, Jura, Task Distribution).

9.3.4 *Role in decision-making*

Looking at the role of CFCs in the process of coordination and decision-making within the administration, a cautionary note is in order. The Federal Council is a small board, and it meets regularly once a week. Thus, the relevance of frequent informal contacts can hardly be overrated. Given the confidentiality shielding all Federal Council activity, one cannot exactly determine the relative importance of working either informally or through cabinet committees. In the present section we therefore first present the routine coordination process in order to obtain another background against which to evaluate the CFC activity.

Standard procedure. Within the federal administration, a bill or any other project is usually prepared by the appropriate office or agency. This can be seen as the first, fundamental structuring of the problem. Still in a preparatory phase, the project is then circulated among all offices potentially concerned. This is called the *pre-reporting* process, for these offices can file a report outlining their views and suggesting changes.

Based on these pre-reports, the initiating office revises the project. It is only at this stage that the department in charge officially places the issue on the Federal Council's agenda, thus leaving the preparatory phase. The new version of the project is then circulated on the department level. This crucial *co-reporting* process allows for comments, suggestions, and objections by the six other departments (i.e. their head). Based on the co-reports, the final version of a project is prepared by the department in charge.

It is then discussed and formally decided upon by the Federal Council in its regular meeting. Thus, if all points of view are adequately respected, and this is often the case, the result of the co-reporting process is the one sanctioned by the Federal Council. In this instance, decision by the Council is a mere formal requirement. Only if substantial differences are not smoothed out by recurring to reporting processes is the Federal Council the actual locus of debate and decision.

Decision-making with CFCs. The information presented here is based on confidential sources. CFCs are a part of the Federal Council's activity, to which no official access is granted, even for scientific purposes. We were thus forced to rely on interviews with people in positions appropriate to yield some intimate personal knowledge on the subject. This, of course, implies that our insights are not based on a rigidly systematic survey, and that they may have to be taken *cum grano salis*.

With regard to the standard procedure, CFC activity does not replace the co-reporting process. It is during the preparatory phase that CFCs, depending on the issues, either replace or complement the regular coordination procedures.

CFC meetings include the three appointed Federal Councillors and, to varying degrees, their top administrators, i.e. the directors of the offices involved. The participation of civil servants may vary according to the specific issues on the agenda.

As to the frequency of meetings, four times a year appears to be a rare maximum. Some CFCs, for intance, have not met at all during the past nine months. Meetings are called by the chairman of the committee, whose staff is also responsible for the administrative components of CFC activity (minutes, etc.).

From the evidence gathered it is safe to conclude that CFC meetings are not held for routine issues. Minor projects and implementation problems are handled through the standard procedure of pre- and co-reporting processes.

CFC activity, then, concerns projects which tackle entire problem areas in a (relatively) new way; projects for new or altered constitutional provisions, or for certain laws of fundamental scope. In those instances, the routine procedure apparently does not suffice, and separate negotiations among the three most concerned departments are needed.

A few selected examples may illustrate the point. Some years ago, the Department of Energy and Transportation prepared proposals intended to handle the fields of energy and transportation. At this time, the two appropriate CFCs met several times. Today, the main issue in the same department is the handling of conceptual problems related to mass media. Consequently, the CFC on Mass Media was established in 1982 and it is active now, whereas Energy and Transportation at present seem to exist on paper only. Similarly, the CFC on Physical Planning had its heyday in the 1970s (when the relevant legislation was under way), and it is today, at least temporarily, de-activated.

The CFC on the Distribution of Tasks does (or rather did) not concern itself with all questions arising in this field. The re-assignment of existing central government activities (e.g. subsidies for low-cost housing) to the federal or the Canton level was evaluated by the designated office in the Department of Justice. Questions were usually settled in bilateral negotiations with the federal level concerned. On the other hand, task distribution problems could arise from new projects or from changes in existing programmes with no immediate concern for the task distribution aspect. It was for these cases that the CFC functioned as a clearing house, enabling other Offices and Departments to have the distributional issues involved in their activity analysed.

An example of a surprisingly influential CFC is the committee on General Economic Policy. Here we find not only the appropriate Federal Councillors and the top administrators of the economically crucial federal offices. Also present is the directorate of the otherwise fairly independent Nationalbank (Federal Reserve). This CFC meets approximately four times a year and it is said to determine definitively the guidelines for Swiss economic policy. The inclusion of the powerful Federal Reserve (responsible for monetary and currency policy) almost lets one suspect that this CFC is a 'shadow cabinet for economic affairs'.

Thus, we are confronted with quite a range of possibilities for the role of CFC in decision-making. The main application, however, is for major projects of rather unprecedented scope. After the passing of the respective bills, CFCs are usually relegated to only formal existence. They still exist, but are not in action unless a new challenge arises. Save for the few CFCs in permanent use, a Committee of the Federal Council is something like a *task force at call*. Seldom used, it is the remnant of busier days, and in the case of new problems on a similar scale, it can be re-activated. We will comment on the usefulness of such institutions in section 9.5.

9.4 Functional equivalents
In 9.3 we examined Swiss cabinet committees with respect to their intra-administrative coordination function. Yet, the executive

branch has to reckon with environmental pressures as well. Cabinet committees can fulfil the task of accomodating various interests outside the administrative realm, especially when ministries and agencies are clientele-oriented. In the present chapter, we argue that this is *not* the case in Switzerland. There are functional equivalents for such a coordination of interests on three levels: (a) for private interest groups; (b) on the federal-Canton dimension; and (c) for partisan political demands.

9.4.1 *Expert commissions*

Expert commissions are a prominent feature of the Swiss political system. Of the some 360 existing commissions, $^4/_5$ are of a permanent nature (Germann, 1981: 14). They are an indispensable element of any legislating process. Germann underscores the importance of the assistance provided by the network of expert commissions to the federal bureaucracy, so that it is referred to as a 'shadow administration' by some. The commissions are well linked to the regular federal administration which holds about ¼ of all seats. On the other hand, representatives of organized private interests occupy some 30 per cent of the commission seats (Germann, 1981: 158).

When establishing an expert commission, the Federal Council has a certain latitude as to its composition. By carefully selecting the 'right' experts, the mandating authority exerts considerable substantive influence (Germann, 1981: 42; Linder, 1979: 201). Yet, representational criteria play a key role (Germann, 1981: 45). All relevant interest groups will be represented in an important commission. A relevant interest group is one which can credibly threaten to oppose a project through a popular referendum in case its demands should not be respected. Thus they can influence legislation at a very early stage. Expert commissions provide an effective channel for the integration of powerful group interests. Hence, they are functional equivalents for comparable processes on the government level.

9.4.2 *Directors' conferences*

Directors' Conferences (*Direktorenkonferenz*) are national meetings of the members of the Canton governments responsible for a certain policy area plus the appropriate federal representative. Directors in this sense are the heads of departments in the governments of Cantons. They are, so to speak, the Canton (state) counterparts of the Federal Councillors. Often the conferences are initiated, organized, or stimulated by federal officials. Table 9.7 demonstrates the wide range of issues covered by this instrument. A

TABLE 9.7
Directors' conferences

		Year	
Policy area	1970	1975	1980
Authorities, Gen. Administration	1	1	1
Administration of Justice, Police	3	3	3
Foreign Affairs	–	–	–
National Defence	1	2	2
Education and Research	1	1	1
Culture, Recreation & Sports	–	–	–
Public Health	1	1	1
Environmental Protection	–	–	1
Social Welfare	1	1	1
Physical Planning	–	–	1
Transportation and Energy	–	–	1
Agriculture	1	1	1
Forestry, Hunting and Fishing	1	1	1
Waters Correction and Avalanche Protection	1	1	1
Industry, Trade and Crafts	1	1	1
Finance	1	1	1
Total	13	14	17

Source: Nüssli (1982: 197).

study of these conferences and of analogous meetings of more specialized bureaucrats holds that they constitute a 'widely spread, differentiated, and highly specialized network of communication, consultation, bargaining, and mutual adjustment' (Tamm, 1982: 2).

Directors' conferences, then, have an important function in facilitating an early consensus, and in anticipating problems posed by the implementation of programmes on lower levels. Discharging the federal apparatus from the task of vertical integration, they are functional equivalents.

9.4.3 *Von Wattenwyl talks*

Besides the integration of particular interests, and the vertical coordination crucial for a federal system, the federal government must also accommodate demands by political parties. The 'von Wattenwyl talks' are a way of harmonizing the Federal Council's and the coalition parties' objectives. They resulted from the combination of two practices begun in the early 1970s. For one, the Federal Council published its own programme in the form of 'guidelines', outlining its priorities over a four-year period. On the other hand, the leaders of the four parties represented in the government met on a regular basis to establish a common stance on the most salient issues. The von Wattenwyl talks, named after the building in which they take place, are usually held four times a year. They include the Federal Council, and the national chairmen and the parliamentary leaders of the four coalition parties. Due to their informal and discreet nature, little is known about their precise contents or of the specificity of agreements reached there. It is certain, however, that the talks serve exactly the purpose of coordinating government objectives with partisan political demands. In this sense, they are functional equivalents too.

9.5 Summary and conclusions
The composition of Committees of the Federal Council (CFCs) is based almost exclusively on substantive criteria. The chairman of a CFC is always the department head most concerned by the CFC's topic. Normally, the two remaining seats are attributed on the same grounds. In politically sensitive areas, and when substantively possible, the third seat may be used to achieve some representational balance.

There is no systematic coverage of policy areas by CFCs. This most likely stems directly from the role in decision-making they play. They are set up in order to shape important and relatively far-reaching projects during their conceptual phase. This implies that CFCs are active at an early stage, before the regular internal coordinating process (co-reports) takes place. CFCs are *not* used to handle routine problems, such as the implementation of programmes.

Since they are not dissolved after their principal tasks have been carried out, i.e. after the conceptual phase, there are CFCs with no immediate purpose. These task forces at call, however, have a function. It is easier and politically more feasible to re-activate an old CFC than to create a new one when needed. Furthermore, CFC can be a valuable instrument in the hands of the Federal Councillor who chairs it. It can be activated at his or her discretion, since the structure is already there and formally sanctioned. Thus, chairmen of CFCs are certainly reluctant to call for their dissolution and so to abandon a potentially useful device for interdepartmental coordination.

The undeniably low saliency of cabinet committees in Switzerland must be attributed to some particularities of the political system. As outlined in the paper, there are functional equivalents for the integration of interests on various levels, viz. the coalition parties, the governments of the Cantons, the organized private interests, all with the respective institutionalized representation mechanisms.

Thus, the principles of direct democracy, of proportional representation and consociationalism, and of federalism all reduce the need for specific intra-cabinet decision-making structures.

In sum, cabinet committees in Switzerland are certainly less prominent than elsewhere. Yet, it would be wrong to conclude from their inconspicuous existence that they are irrelevant. On the contrary (and to our own surprise) we found that CFCs play a more important role in the decision-making process than initially suspected. In this sense, Swiss cabinet committees certainly warrant the political scientist's attention.

Notes

1. Law on Administrative Organization, Art. 17: 'The Federal Council can appoint among its members commissions for certain affairs; it determines their mandate and orders the procedure. The commissions prepare deliberations and decisions of the Federal Council. The other members of the Federal Council are informed by way of minutes.' (Translation by the authors.)

2. Both initiative and referendum are among the most typical features of the Swiss political system. They have thoroughly shaped the modes and structures of decision-making. Initiatives are a way of forcing an otherwise neglected issue into the political arena, or of emphasizing a particular position in an ongoing policy-formulating process (Delley, 1978; Sigg, 1978; Werder, 1978). An initiative must be supported by 100,000 citizens (i.e. approximatively 2.6 per cent of the electorate). The demand for a referendum must be carried by 50,000 citizens (1.3 per cent) and it is usually directed against a Federal Law deemed to violate the interest of a particular group (Neidhart, 1970).

3. For a better understanding of the Federal Council's position one might picture the authority of the US President, rather than being entrusted to one individual, being invested collectively in a seven-member board.

4. The federal government took part in the resolution of the Jura conflict as a mediator. The creation of a new Canton is, legally, no matter of the federal government. Admission to the Confederation was granted to the Canton of Jura by a popular vote in 1978. Yet, the matter was so delicate (and, at times, threatening to upset the stability of the federal system) that the Federal Council sought and received some reconciliatory influence (cf. Campbell, 1982).

References

Amtliches Bulletin der Bundesversammlung, Nationalrat (1976).

Bericht Huber (1971) Bericht und Gesetzesentwurf der Expertenkommission für die Totalrevision des Bundesgesetzes über die Organisation der Bundesverwaltung. Bern.

Bundesblatt der Schweizerischen Eidgenossenschaft (1975).

Campbell, David B. (1982) 'Nationalism, Religion and the Social Bases of Conflict in the Swiss Jura', in Stein Rokkan and Derek W. Urwin (eds), *The Politics of Territorial Identity. Studies in European Regionalism*. Beverly Hills: Sage.

Delley, Jean-Daniel (1978) *L'Initiative Populaire en Suisse: Mythe et Realité de la Démocratie Directe*. Lausanne: L'age d'homme.

Germann, Raimund (1981), *Ausserparlamentarische Kommissionen: Die Milizverwaltung des Bundes*. Bern: Paul Haupt.

Homann, Benno (1982) 'Das Konkordanzsystem der Schweiz: Kritik und Alternativen konkordanztheoretischer Ansätze', *Politische Vierteljahresschrift*, 23: 418–39.

Kriesi, Hanspeter (1981) *Entscheidungsstrukturen und Entscheidungsprozesse in der Schweizer Politik*. Frankfurt: Campus.

Neidhart, Leonhard (1970) *Plebiszit und Pluralitäre Demokratie: Eine Analyse der Funktion des Schweizerischen Gesetzesreferendums*. Bern: Francke.

Nüssli, Kurt (1982) 'Föderalismus in der Schweiz: Konzepte, Indikatoren, Daten'. Unveröffentlichte Dissertation, Universität Zürich.

Rüegg, Erwin (1982) 'Regierbarkeit durch Konkordanz?: Konzepte und Indikatoren zur Konkordanzdemokratie'. Unveröffentlichte Dissertation, Universität Zürich.

Sigg, Oswald (1978) *Die eidgenössischen Volksinitiativen 1892–1939*. Einsiedeln: Benziger.

Tamm, Nikolaus (1982) *Kooperation im Schweizer Bundesstaat: Die Konferenzen der Fachstellen des Bundes und der Kantone*. Riehen: Forschungsinstitut für Föderalismus und Regionalstrukturen.

Werder, Hans (1978) *Die Bedeutung der Volksinitiative in der Nachkriegszeit*. Bern: Francke.

Appendix 9.1 **Selected changes in departmental composition**

TABLE 9.A.1
CFC on Military Matters: Third Seat

Department	Year					
	1970	1973	1974		1982	1983
EVED	————————————					
EJPD			————————————————————			
EVD						——

TABLE 9.A.2
CFC on Agriculture: Third Seat

Department	Year					
	1970	1973	1974		1982	1983
EJPD	————————————					
EDI			————————————————			
EMD						———————

TABLE 9.A.3
CFC on Finance Policy: Third Seat

Department	Year						
	1978	1979	1980	1981	1982	1983	1984
EVED	———————						
EMD			————————————————				
EJPD						—————————————	

Appendix 9.2 Departmental composition of CFCs

CFC	1970	1971	1972	1973	1974	1975	1976	1977	1978	1979	1980	1981	1982	1983	1984
Railroad Matters	EVED	EVED	EVED	EVED	EVED	EVED	EVED	EVED	EVED	EVED					
	EFD	EFD	EFD	EFD	EFD	EFD	EFD	EFD	ᶜEFD	EFD					
	EDA	EDA	EDA	EDA	EDA	EDA	EDA	EDA	EDA	EDA					
Foreign Affairs	EDA	EDA	EDA	EDA	EDA	EDA	EDA	EDA	EDA	EDA	EDA	EDA	EDA	EDA	EDA
	EVD	EVD	EVD	EVD	EVD	EVD	EVD	EVD	EVD	EVD	EVD	EVD	EVD	EVD	EVD
	EFD	EFD	EJPD	EJPD	EJPD	EJPD	EJPD	EJPD	EJPD	EJPD	EJPD	EJPD	EJPD	EJPD	EJPD
Military Matters	EMD	EMD	EMD	EMD	EMD	EMD	EMD	EMD	EMD	EMD	EMD	EMD	EMD	EMD	EMD
	EVED	EVED	EVED	EVED	EJPD	EJPD	EJPD	EJPD	EJPD	EJPD	EJPD	EJPD	EJPD	EVD	EVD
	EFD	EFD	EFD	EFD	EFD	EFD	EFD	EFD	EFD	EFD	EFD	EFD	EFD	EFD	EFD
Science and Research	EDI	EDI	EDI	EDI	EDI	EDI	EDI	EDI	EDI	EDI	EDI	EDI	EDI	EDI	EDI
	EVD	EVD	EVD	EVD	EVD	EVD	EVD	EVD	EVD	EVD	EVD	EVD	EVD	EVD	EVD
	EDA	EDA	EDA	EDA	EDA	EDA	EDA	EDA	EDA	EDA	EDA	EDA	EDA	EDA	EDA
Agriculture	EVD	EVD	EVD	EVD	EVD	EVD	EVD	EVD	EVD	EVD	EVD	EVD	EVD	EVD	EVD
	EFD	EFD	EFD	EFD	EFD	EFD	EFD	EFD	EFD	EFD	EFD	EFD	EFD	EFD	EFD
	EJPD	EJPD	EJPD	EJPD	EDI	EDI	EDI	EDI	EDI	EDI	EDI	EDI	EDI	EMD	EMD
Transportation	EVED	EVED	EVED	EVED	EVED	EVED	EVED	EVED	EVED	EVED	EVED	EVED	EVED	EVED	EVED
	EDI	EDI	EDI	EDI	EDI	EDI	EDI	EDI	EDI	EDI	EDI	EDI	EDI	EDI	EDI/EFD
	EJPD	EJPD	EJPD	EJPD	EJPD	EJPD	EJPD	EJPD	EJPD	EJPD	EJPD	EJPD	EJPD	EJPD	EJPD
Physical Planning	EJPD	EJPD	EJPD	EJPD	EJPD	EJPD	EJPD	EJPD	EJPD	EJPD	EJPD	EJPD	EJPD	EJPD	EJPD
	EDI	EDI	EDI	EDI	EVED	EVED	EVED	EVED	EVED	EVED	EVED	EVED	EVED	EVED	EVED
	EVD	EVD	EVD	EVD	EVD	EVD	EVD	EVD	EVD	EDI	EDI	EDI	EDI	EDI	EDI

Appendix 9.2 Departmental composition of CFCs (continued)

CFC	1970	1971	1972	1973	1974	1975	1976	1977	1978	1979	1980	1981	1982	1983	1984
Energy					EVED	EVED	EVED	EVED	EVED	EVED	EVED	EVED	EVED	EVED	EVED
					EVD	EVD	EVD	EVD	EVD	EVD	EVD	EVD	EVD	EVD	EVD
					EDI	EDI	EDI	EDI	EDI	EDI	EDI	EDI	EDI	EDI	EDI
Economy and Finance	EVD	EVD	EVD	EVD	EVD	EVD	EVD	EVD							
	EFD	EFD	EFD	EFD	EFD	EFD	EFD	EFD							
	EDA	EDA	EDA	EDA	EDA	EDA	EDA	EDA							
Foreign Trade									EVD	EVD	EVD	EVD	EVD	EVD	EVD
									EDA	EDA	EDA	EDA	EDA	EDA	EDA
									EFD	EFD	EFD	EFD	EFD	EFD	EFD
General Economic Policy									EVD	EVD	EVD	EVD	EVD	EVD	EVD
									EFD	EFD	EFD	EFD	EFD	EFD	EFD
									EJPD	EJPD	EJPD	EJPD	EJPD	EMD	EMD
Finance Policy									EFD	EFD	EFD	EFD	EFD	EFD	EFD
									EDI	EDI	EDI	EDI	EDI	EDI	EDI
									EVED	EVED	EMD	EMD	EMD	EJPD	EJPD
Jura Affairs											EJPD	EJPD	EJPD	EJPD	
											EFD	EFD	EFD	EFD	
											EMD	EMD	EMD	EMD	

Appendix 9.2 Departmental composition of CFCs (continued)

CFC	1970	1971	1972	1973	1974	1975	1976	1977	1978	1979	1980	1981	1982	1983	1984
Federal/Canton Distribution of Tasks											EJPD EFD EMD	EJPD EFD EMD	EJPD EFD EMD	EJPD EFD EMD	EJPD EFD EMD
Mass Media														EVED EDI EJPD	EVED EDI EJPD

Abbreviations:
- EDA: Eidg. Departement für Auswärtiges = Foreign Affairs.
- EDI: Eidg. Departement des Innern = Interior.
- EJPD: Eidg. Justiz- u. Polizeidepartement = Justice and Police.
- EMD: Eidg. Militärdepartement = Military.
- EFD: Eidg. Finanz- u. Zolldepartement = Finance and Customs.
- EVD: Eidg. Volkswirtschaftsdepartement = National Economy.
- EVED: Eidg. Verkehrs- u. Energiewirtschaftsdepartement = Transportation and Energy.

Index

Notes on contributors

Rudy B. Andeweg is Lecturer in Political Science at Leyden University. He has co-authored a number of articles and books on Netherlands politics and electoral change. In 1982 and 1983 he was an assistant to the Netherlands Government's Commissioner for Administrative Reform. In 1985 he received a Huygens fellowship to prepare a study of cabinet decision-making.

Colin Campbell, SJ, is Martin University Professor of Philosophy and Politics at Georgetown University in Washington DC. He is the co-author of *The Super-bureaucrats: Structure and Behaviour in Central Agencies, The Contemporary Canadian Legislative System*, and *Parliament, Policy and Representation*. His most recent book is *Governments under Stress: Political Executives and Key Bureaucrats in Washington, London and Ottawa*.

Jørgen Grønnegård Christensen is Professor of Public Administration at the Institute of Political Science, University of Aarhus. He worked for some years in the Danish Ministry of Defence.

Ulrich Klöti obtained a PhD in Sociology and Economics from Berne in 1972. He studied Political Science in Princeton and Ann Arbor before he worked as a personal secretary of the Swiss Chancellor for seven years. Since 1980 he has been Professor of Political Science at the University of Zurich. He is President of the Swiss Political Science Association for 1984–6.

Brian W. Hogwood is a Lecturer in Politics at the University of Strathclyde. He is author or co-author of *Government and Shipbuilding, Regional Government in England, Policy Dynamics, Policy Analysis for the Real World* and *The Pathology of Public Policy*. His research interests are in the area of public policy, particularly industrial policy and the analysis of different types of policy change.

Thomas T. Mackie is Lecturer in Politics at the University of Strathclyde. He is the co-author of *The International Almanac of Electoral History* and of the *Europe Votes* series. His current research interests include elections and party systems in western countries and the comparative study of political executives.

Hans-Jakob Mosimann has a PhD in Law from the University of Zurich and an MA in Political Science from Virginia Tech. He is a research assistant at the University of Zurich.

Patrick Weller is Professor of Public Policy in the School of Social and Industrial Administration at Griffith University, Queensland. He is a graduate of Exeter College, Oxford and the Australian National University. He is editor of *Politics*, the journal of the Australian Political Studies Association. Among many books and articles, he is co-author of *Treasury Control in Australia* (1976), *Politics and Policy in Australia* (1979), *Can Ministers Cope?* (1981) and author of *First Among Equals: Prime Ministers in Westminster Systems* (1985).